THE CLERK'S
PROLOGUE AND TALE

belle et en point de marier et le
frere dicelle fille qui auoit enui
ron sept ans · Comment ledit
marquis dist a sa femme griscl
dis quil falloit quil preist au
tre femme quelle · et comment
il la renuoia chies son pere tou
te nue excepte tant seulement
vne poure chemise · Et comment
iamcole son pere luy vint au de
uant qui luy bailla ses poures
vestemens quil auoit garde ·

THE
CLERK'S PROLOGUE
AND TALE

FROM THE CANTERBURY TALES BY
GEOFFREY CHAUCER

*Edited with Introduction, Notes
and Glossary by*

JAMES WINNY

CAMBRIDGE
UNIVERSITY PRESS

Published by the Press Syndicate of the University of Cambridge
The Pitt Building, Trumpington Street, Cambridge CB2 1RP
40 West 20th Street, New York, NY 10011–4211, USA
10 Stamford Road, Oakleigh, Victoria 3166, Australia

ISBN 0 521 04632 7

First published 1966
Eighth printing 1992

Printed in Great Britain at the
University Press, Cambridge

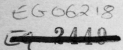

For my daughter

DEBORAH

CONTENTS

ACKNOWLEDGEMENTS

The editor wishes to thank the Bibliothèque Nationale at Paris for permission to reproduce a miniature from *Le Livre Griseldis* as frontispiece, and the Librarian of the University Library at Cambridge for the photograph of the map of Piedmont by Giacomo Gastaldi, reproduced on page 66.

The miniature shows Griselda, covered more adequately than the text suggests, returning to her father's house after being rejected and stripped of possessions by the Marquis. The chapter-heading above the miniature runs:

'Comment ledit / marquis dist a sa femme grisel / dis quil failloit quil preist au / tre femme quelle et comment / il la renvoia chiez son pere tou / te nue excepte tant seulement / une povre chemise Et comment / Janicole son pere lui vint au de / vant qui lui bailla ses povres / vestemens quil avoit garde.'

(How the said Marquis told his wife Griselda that he must take another wife, and how he sent her back to her father's house, naked apart from a mean shift; and how her father Janicola came out to her and gave her back the humble clothes which he had looked after.)

INTRODUCTION

The third fragment of *The Canterbury Tales* consists of three linked stories, told by the Wife of Bath, the Friar, and the Summoner. It is followed by a shorter fragment, in which the Clerk and the Merchant tell their tales. Together, the five stories make up a single dramatic sequence. *The Friar's Tale* and *The Summoner's Tale* are sparked off by a quarrel which breaks out during the Wife of Bath's already eventful Prologue, leaving both pilgrims angrily waiting to take revenge through libellous stories. After this caustic interlude and a break in the narrative commentary, Chaucer returns to the issue of sovereignty in marriage which the Wife of Bath had raised. The Clerk, who makes some pointed references to this arch-feminist in his Envoy (line 1170 below), tells a story of wifely patience which might be intended to shame her into modesty and submissiveness. The Wife is not allowed to reply to this reproach, but the theme of wifely behaviour is taken up by the Merchant, a man recently and unhappily married, who finds the tale of 'Grisildis grete pacience' cruelly ironic. His own story illustrates the cynical view of marriage which a short but painful experience of 'wives cursednesse' has forced upon him. Thus all five stories are connected, by arising out of an event in the previous tale or through their subject-matter; and of the three tales on marriage the story of patient Griselda, told by the Clerk, occupies a position between the Wife's militant feminism and the Merchant's cynically contemptuous attitude to matrimony.

Because these three tales present contrasting views of

1

married life, it has been argued that Chaucer was arranging a serious debate which ends in the generous solution proposed in *The Franklin's Tale*. The Clerk's allusions to the Wife of Bath, and the Merchant's reference to Griselda, prove that a conscious and purposeful relationship exists between the three works. This does not mean that the tales are to be read primarily as contributions to a debate on marriage. It is not the stories which formulate different attitudes towards the married state so much as the individual pilgrims who tell them. The Wife of Bath sets out her belief in womanly sovereignty with much greater energy in her extended Prologue than in the fairy-tale which follows. Similarly, without the Merchant's admission of his wife's 'passing crueltee' in his Prologue, it would be more difficult to recognize his Tale as a calculated attack upon the whole institution of marriage. The links, and the satirical Envoy to *The Clerk's Tale*, suggest a closer relationship between the tales of the so-called Marriage Group than the stories themselves justify. Separated from this setting, they are seen as a group of miscellaneous tales dealing variously with the perennial subjects of love, marriage, and sexual intrigue, and enclosed within a frame which attributes a common interest to them all. While it remains true that the larger significance of Chaucer's work is obscured when the tales are detached from their setting, it may also happen that the narrative frame gives a false emphasis to the individual stories, by requiring them to illustrate a theme not central to their own purposes. This is especially true when the tale seems not to have been written as part of the connected sequence, but drafted into the design of *The Canterbury Tales* at the most appropriate point. *The Clerk's Tale* is such a case.

Some disparity between the style of the Tale and the character of the teller is apparent from the outset. The Clerk is not one of the more impressive pilgrims. Unlike the gaudy Wife of Bath or the gaily dressed Squire, he does not force himself upon attention by unusual manner or appearance, but remains as reserved and unobtrusive as Chaucer himself. Again like the poet, he has to be roused from scholarly absorption when it is his turn to continue the entertainment. But although the Host—a sure judge of social importance—wastes little respect upon the Clerk, the poet finds at least one point to praise unreservedly:

> Noght o word spak he moore than was neede,
> And that was seyd in forme and reverence,
> And short and quik and ful of hy sentence.

Such economy of speech could be expected of a scholar, whose lifelong association with Latin might well encourage him to speak pithily. But this ideal of scholarly terseness seems to have attracted Chaucer as a stylistic quality which, by the date of the *General Prologue*, he had mastered in his own use of language. The Clerk is being praised for the quality which Chaucer had now adopted as the standard of his poetic style. The *General Prologue* abounds in terse, compact observations, 'short and quik' and swept clear of merely decorative terms. There every phrase, every adjective and descriptive term is made to justify its place in the sentence by working. The result can be felt in statements that are as hard and definite as rounded pebbles:

> His heed was balled, that shoon as any glas,
> And eek his face, as he hadde been enoint.

3

Such a standard of clear, forceful writing, obtained by
sacrificing courtly elegance and rhetorical artifice, seems
to have been considered earlier in Chaucer's career, only
to be rejected as comic. At the end of his instructive
lecture in *The House of Fame*, the Eagle preens himself
on his ability to speak 'lewedly to a lewed man', that is,
in simple everyday language. In fact, the Eagle's lecture
is full of rhetorical forms and figures, and its vocabulary
would strain the understanding of an unlearned audience.
Here, evidently, the notion of using colloquial English in
poetry is introduced only as a donnish joke; but when,
before allowing him to begin his Tale, the Host warns the
Clerk not to use forms of speech beyond a common man's
grasp, Chaucer is mixing a serious purpose with his
playfulness:

> Youre terms, youre colours, and youre figures,
> Keepe hem in stoor til so be that ye endite
> Heigh style, as whan that men to kinges write.
> Speketh so pleyn at this time, we yow preye,
> That we may understonde what ye seye. (16–20)

By instructing the Clerk to tell his story in simple colloquial terms, the Host is in effect dictating the style in
which Chaucer should write the Tale which follows.
Devices of this kind, which make Chaucer appear a mere
reporter, unable to modify the embarrassingly frank or
vulgar language of his own pilgrims, appear more than
once in *The Canterbury Tales*. Chaucer issues a pre-
liminary caution in the *General Prologue*, pleading with
his readers,

> N'arette it nat my vileynie,
> Though that I pleynly speke in this mateere;

meaning that if his tales happen to be outspoken, his hearers should not mistake him for a coarse and ill-bred person. As narrator of the whole series, Chaucer feels obliged to repeat verbatim all that he hears, however uncouth. He puts up the same comic argument before *The Miller's Tale*, again insisting that he must recount the story just as it was told, 'or elles falsen som of my mateere'. In both passages the stylistic justification is partly ironic. The reader knows that the pilgrims are Chaucer's brain-children, and that his fear of distorting the truth by polite censorship is a solemn joke. Yet this joke overlies a serious intention. The racy and uncourtly expressions used in many of the fabliaux call for some apology, as Chaucer tacitly acknowledges by trying to shift responsibility from himself to his characters, but this is none the less the language in which he has chosen to tell the tales. Behind this comic smokescreen we see Chaucer purposefully creating figures and events who rely for their reality upon the vital energies of popular speech. The traditions of courtly poetry which had previously influenced his style no longer answer all his imaginative needs, and to make his new style acceptable he tries to suggest that the pilgrims are speaking, and not himself. When the Host demands a tale in plain English, it seems that the Clerk has no alternative but to adopt a popular manner of speech. In fact, through the Host, Chaucer is laying down the conditions of his own final style.

Yet the Clerk appears to ignore his instructions. Despite the Host's strictures he offers the company a story taken from one of the most scholarly of medieval European authors, freely admitting that the original tale is cast in the lofty style expressly forbidden by the Host. Moreover, as soon as he embarks on the Tale, Chaucer seems to forget the literary standard attributed to the Clerk in the *General Prologue*, making no attempt to give the narrative the dramatic compression which the portrait leads us to expect. Neither the form nor the manner of the tale suggests intellectual quickness in the narrator. Otiose phrases and pleonasms occur throughout—'yong of age', 'seyde as ye shul heere', 'fortune or aventure', 'seyn with mannes ye'. Expressions which fill up a line without adding substantially to the sense are also common: 'out of drede', 'certeyn', 'it is no nay', 'as I gesse'. Many of these nerveless phrases, and the general lack of urgency in the narrative, may reflect the difficulty of fitting the story into a complex stanza-form of seven lines, rhyming in irregular sequence. But if Chaucer could accept the diffusion of narrative which rhyme-royal forced upon him, that was because the stylistic qualities ascribed to the Clerk were not yet urging him away from an essentially lyrical form towards the bold simplicity of the couplet. Few stanzas of *The Clerk's Tale* develop the story very far, or display the 'short and quik' utterance which Chaucer admired in his pilgrim. Walter's leisurely address to Janicula at a crucial moment of the story conveys no sense of momentous occasion:

> 'Thou lovest me, I woot it wel certeyn,
> And art my feithful lige man ybore;
> And al that liketh me, I dar wel seyn
> It liketh thee, and specially therfore
> Tel me that point that I have seyd bifore,
> If that thou wolt unto that purpos drawe,
> To take me as for thy sone-in-law.'

(309–15)

Instead of narrative drive, the lines evoke a mood of unhurried dignity which the events of the tale never seriously disturb. The quiet tone and pace of *The Clerk's Tale* are obviously appropriate to its courtly subject. Related in the spare, compact style employed in *The Pardoner's Tale*, the story would lose the gentle atmosphere which is Griselda's proper context. Pathos and womanly sentiment do not invite matter-of-fact treatment. The fact remains, however, that Chaucer put this tale into the mouth of a pilgrim whose direct and economical mode of speech had attracted special comment. It seems reasonable to assume that, had the tale been written after the composition of the *General Prologue*, its style would have matched the description given in his portrait. But it is questionable whether, at that date, the subject-matter of *The Clerk's Tale* would have made any strong appeal to Chaucer.

The origins of the Griselda story are a good deal more remote than either Boccaccio or Petrarch, through whom the tale descended to Chaucer, could have realized. Behind these sophisticated forms of the story lies the folk-tale of the Patient Wife, of which independent versions survive in the ballad *Fair Annie* and the lay *Le Freine*. Behind the folk-tale can be discerned a still earlier form of the story, centring upon a liaison between a mortal woman and a supernatural being which can only become permanent if the woman observes the condition imposed by her lover at the beginning of their relationship. In the myth of Cupid and Psyche she is forbidden to see the face of her lover, who visits her only during darkness. The heroine of the folk-tale must agree to be subservient to all her lord's wishes, accepting his decisions even when they are cruelly unfeeling, and making no protest when she is publicly humiliated by his choosing a new consort. The reward of her constancy is to win her supernatural lover as a husband whom she need no longer fear to lose.

The interest of the folk-tale lies chiefly in the encounter of mortal with unearthly, and in the heroine's successful carrying out of an almost impossible requirement. We meet this motif elsewhere; in *All's Well that Ends Well*, for instance, where the nobleman Bertram refuses to acknowledge the humbly born wife forced upon him until she has fulfilled the terms of his seemingly unfeasible condition. The hero's reluctance to marry, a feature of the story repeated in *The Clerk's Tale* and *Le Freine*, probably derives from an earlier version of the tale in which he featured as a supernatural being, understandably unwilling to bind himself to a mortal partner. The conditions accepted by Griselda—complete submission, unruffled patience, and constancy—do not seem unduly difficult; but the tests which follow require her to stifle her deepest instincts as a mother, and to overcome the keenest womanly resentment to serve at the marriage-feast of her successor. To achieve her end, she must possess the superhuman power of endurance that will outwit a lover who has all the advantages of fairy nature, persisting unchanged until he confesses himself beaten by her constancy.

Like other folk-stories, the tale of the Patient Wife underwent modifications as it was absorbed into a conscious literary tradition. The most obvious change deprived the story of its unearthly elements. The fairy lover was rationalized into a mortal man, and the disparity

8

between him and the heroine, formerly one of kind, now dwindled to one of social class. He became a nobleman, she a peasant like Griselda or a foundling like Le Freine. With the loss of its supernatural element the story became in some ways more credible, but on the other hand the motives which explained the behaviour of both hero and heroine had been removed. Chaucer's awkward attempts to account for Walter's cruel treatment of Griselda show how the story suffered by losing a hero whose imperviousness was part of his supernatural character. The poet had not only to devise some explanation of a nobleman's wantonly sadistic trial of his wife's fortitude and constancy. He had also to give the tale another basis of interest; not in the struggle of a mortal woman to win a husband by fulfilling impossibly difficult conditions, but in the drama of human feeling which her uncomprehending constancy involved.

This was the aspect of the Griselda story which seems to have attracted Chaucer. In all essentials, the tale which he recounts through the Clerk came from Petrarch, whose *Epistolae Seniles* offers a basis of comparison with Chaucer's version of the story. Although the Clerk does not admit a second debt, it is evident that Chaucer also used a French translation of Petrarch's tale, often preferring its readings. We thus have two checks upon Chaucer's handling of the story, which enable us to follow his reshaping of incidents and varying of mood, as well as his generally close adherence to the text of one or both of his sources. Where he changes or innovates, it is usually with the object of deepening the pathos of Griselda's situation, and of working upon the tender feelings of his audience. His account of the sergeant's first visit to

Griselda is typical of this shift towards sentiment. The heroine of *Le Livre Griseldis* remains silent and apparently unmoved throughout. 'And with composed expression', the tale runs in this version, 'she took her child, and looked at her for a little while, and kissed and blessed her, making the sign of the cross, and gave her to the sergeant' (see note on line 550). Chaucer makes much more of the episode, improvising freely and giving Griselda a long and pathetic speech where her French counterpart surrenders her child without comment. With the change from impersonal narrative to direct speech the scene comes to life, but comparison with *Le Livre Griseldis* shows how far Chaucer departs from the austere spirit of the tale he is following:

> And thus she seyde in hire benigne vois,
> 'Fareweel my child! I shal thee nevere see.
> But sith I thee have marked with the crois
> Of thilke Fader—blessed moote he be!—
> That for us deyde upon a crois of tree,
> Thy soule, litel child, I him bitake,
> For this night shaltow dyen for my sake...' (554–60)

> And to the sergeant mekely she saide,
> 'Have heer again youre litel yonge maide.' (566–7)

The pathetic feeling which Chaucer evokes so successfully in these stanzas typifies his courtly sophistication of the folk-tale which provided the basic form of the Griselda story. Emotions which would have been entirely alien to the folk-tale, and which neither Petrarch nor his French translator attempts to arouse, become for Chaucer a major concern of the story. His unconvincing attempt to account for Walter's inhuman treatment of Griselda is similarly foreign to the traditions of the tale, and

without parallel in either of his two literary sources.
'Ther been folk of swich condicion,' he remarks, improvising freely,

> That whan they have a certein purpos take,
> They kan nat stinte of hire entencion,
> But, right as they were bounden to a stake,
> They wol nat of that firste purpos slake. (702–5)

The marquis, in Chaucer's view, is possessed by an
irrational compulsion which he cannot shake off, and the
helpless victim of his 'wikke usage' is a bewildered
creature who can no more understand Walter's purposes
than he can himself. Although Chaucer follows the usual
form of the tale in describing how the marquis exacts a
promise of uncomplaining constancy as a condition of
marriage, he then seems to disregard the incident, as
though not recognizing the close link between Griselda's
promise and the trials which follow. 'Be ye redy with
good herte,' Walter asks her at this crucial meeting,

> 'To al my lust, and that I frely may,
> As me best thinketh, do yow laughe or smerte,
> And nevere ye to grucche it, night ne day?
> And eek whan I sey "ye", ne sey nat "nay",
> Neither by word ne frowning contenance?
> Swere this, and heere I swere oure alliance.' (352–7)

For Chaucer as for Petrarch, the significance of the episode
seems to have fallen out of sight. During her sufferings
Griselda never reflects that there may be some connection
between these trials and the promise made on her wedding-
day. She accepts her grief and abasement without hope of
reward, not as a woman consciously steeling herself against
the natural impulse to protest, but as a wife whose
gentleness and humility allow her no other course than

submission. Petrarch might see Griselda as an emblem of the soul patiently undergoing the purifying ordeals of worldly tribulation. For Chaucer, whether consciously or not, she is rather the embodiment of an exalted courtly ideal of unfailing graciousness and well-mannered restraint.

With this shift of emphasis *The Clerk's Tale* emerges from Chaucer's hands as a tender story whose climaxes are moments of deep human feeling, not of dramatic surprise. The taking of Griselda's children, her plea for a single garment when she is dismissed from the palace, and her reunion with the children whom she supposed dead, are treated as opportunities for making a heavily sentimental appeal to the reader's sympathies. Chaucer's comment on the last of these episodes,

> O which a pitous thing it was to se
> Hir swowning, and hire humble vois to heere! (1086–7)

indicates the kind of emotional response he is seeking to arouse; and his remark that the weeping courtiers could hardly bear to watch the scene shows how poignantly he expects a sensitive audience to be moved. To modern taste he may appear too insistently pathetic, and over-committed to the literary concepts of 'reuthe' and 'pitee' which provide a plaintive undertone to his story. The satirical portrait of the Prioress in the *General Prologue*, who is careful to display her 'tendre herte' by weeping over dead mice and anguished lapdogs, proves that Chaucer was not to remain uncritically attached to the modish conventions of courtly feeling. His singleness of outlook in *The Clerk's Tale* is uncharacteristic. In *Troilus and Criseyde*, to take the most prominent and accomplished of

his courtly poems, the purity and chivalrous idealism
of Troilus are offset by Pandarus, who has a more
realistic respect for facts and a truer judgement of human
impulse. A similar balance of extremes is found in *The
Parliament of Fowls*, where the lower orders of birds—
duck, goose and cuckoo—are allowed to ridicule the
refined manners of the formel eagle and her noble suitors.
In *The Clerk's Tale* there is no such counterpoise to the
mood of delicate fantasy, and no bustling physical energy
to offset Chaucer's appeal to feeling through the sad
lyrical beauty of his tale.

This singleness of attention appears again in Chaucer's
handling of the humbler figures of the story, and of their
rustic background. The hamlet where Griselda lives with
her father is not described with the sharply particular eye
that observes the yard 'enclosed al aboute with stikkes',
where Chauntecleer lords it over his seven paramours.
The comment, 'of site delitable', is left to suggest its
pleasant character, with no further details. Janicula's
poverty is dignified by being associated with the Nativity,
and the hardships of Griselda's life are described allusively
through images which suggest a biblical rather than a
medieval English background. In the account of her first
meeting with the marquis this effect is particularly
marked:

> And she set doun hir water pot anon
> Biside the thresshfold, in an oxes stalle,
> And doun upon hir knes she gan to falle.   (290–2)

Lack of education and of contact with polite society does
not prevent her from speaking with unaffected courtesy
and womanly grace. Lesser characters of the Tale without

13

claim to courtly rank have the same gentleness of address. Even the cruel sergeant, whose forbidding appearance accords with his sinister reputation, apologizes to Griselda in the cultured manner of a gentleman concerned at her distress:

> 'Madame,' he seyde, 'ye moote foryeve it me,
> Though I do thing to which I am constreyned.
> Ye been so wys that ful wel knowe ye
> That lordes heestes mowe nat been yfeyned.
> They mowe wel been biwailled or compleyned.' (526–30)

His quietly modulated speech characterizes the idiom of the Tale. The same unhurried rhythms move through dialogue and narrative, in language which never strains after flamboyance but relies upon simple evocative terms for its emotional effect:

> And in hir barm this litel child she leyde
> With ful sad face, and gan the child to blisse,
> And lulled it, and after gan it kisse.　(551–3)

This almost monosyllabic clarity and homeliness of style shows how little Chaucer conceded to the possible artificiality of courtly taste. Griselda's story is told in language which matches her own quiet strength of purpose and wistful charm—or rather, which is the source of those qualities. Had Chaucer introduced an occasional flash of comic irony he would have shattered the enchantment of the mood which his poetry holds in its net.

But the Prologue and Envoy which enclose the Tale proper offer a direct contrast of style. The boisterous remarks of the Host which bring the Clerk out of retirement, and the sardonic advice to the Wife of Bath and her tribe which rounds off the story, are as remote from the lyrical mood of the tale as street-cries from madrigals. The Host, with his practical man's contempt for the niceties of scholarship and his downright manner of speech—

> For Goddes sake, as beth of bettre cheere!
> It is no time for to studien heere.
> Telle us som myrie tale, by youre fey! (7–9)

—would find no place in the soft-spoken world of Griselda's marquisate. In the Prologue the Clerk submits to the Host's badinage with a polite deference that might explain his interest in the Tale, but in the Envoy he switches to a strongly vernacular idiom and becomes bitingly satirical:

> Ye archewives, stondeth at defense,
> Sin ye be strong as is a greet camaille;
> Ne suffreth nat that men yow doon offense...
> Ay clappeth as a mille, I yow consaille. (1195–200)

Here Chaucer's writing generates the colloquial energy that is the hallmark of his final style. In place of the courtly terms and lyrical cadences of the Tale, he turns to language with the rough immediacy of popular speech, exploiting idiomatic expressions which carry the stamp of everyday reality. The description of Griselda's bridal journey upon a horse 'snow-whit and wel ambling' gives the event a fairy-tale quality which the whole tale supports. The Clerk's advice to wives at the end of the Tale, 'Beth nat bidaffed for youre innocence', has the effect of a sudden and noisy change of gear. From a lofty ideal of truth and gentleness we are flung back into a sarcastic controversy over sovereignty in marriage, initiated by the Wife of Bath earlier in the pilgrimage.

This marked contrast of style and outlook suggests that *The Clerk's Tale* was written before Chaucer conceived the plan of unifying a great body of unrelated tales through the device of the Canterbury pilgrimage. Some of the tales were clearly in existence before the date of the *General Prologue*, and were then fitted into the design where occasion offered, not always very plausibly. To introduce an older tale by means of a head-link or prologue was not difficult, but the matching of tale to pilgrim presented a greater problem. Would the unworldly Clerk, whom the Host sees as absorbed in the intellectual subtleties of scholarship, have told the pathetic courtly story of Griselda? Since the Tale was admittedly borrowed from the worthy clerk 'Fraunceys Petrak', it might seem so; and it can always be claimed that an unexpected story throws light on the inner personality of the pilgrim concerned. But we have already seen that in one vital respect *The Clerk's Tale* refuses to be associated with the pilgrim described in the *General Prologue*. The curious disparity between the form of speech attributed to him and the actual form of *The Clerk's Tale* is evidence that the Tale was not written with the Clerk in mind, but assigned to him out of the stock of earlier stories which were absorbed into *The Canterbury Tales*.

It could be argued that Chaucer was at liberty to return to an earlier style in order to give variety to his work. But style is not an outer garment unrelated to the body of poetry beneath. It is part of the means by which a great poet gives substance to an imaginative view of life, and an intrinsic part of what he creates. For Chaucer as for Shakespeare, the style and subject-matter of the final period are closely associated, as parts of a single expression. Not only the vocabulary and manner of *The Clerk's Tale* distinguish it from the comic stories of Chaucer's final phase. His later work depicts human affairs from the standpoint of an ironically detached spectator, holding sentimental feeling at arm's length where *The Clerk's Tale* seeks to involve the reader in pathetic emotions. In the comic tales this ironic commentary does more than illuminate the events and characters of the story from within. It embodies an awareness of double standards which enables the poet to keep his writing —and even his own person—in critical perspective, using an astringent wit to check any movement towards excess of feeling. *The Clerk's Tale* lacks this critical depth. Only in the Envoy does Chaucer admit the charming unreality of his story by making the speaker warn his audience against expecting such constancy of their own wives:

> No wedded man so hardy be t'assaille
> His wives pacience in trust to finde
> Grisildis, for in certein he shal faille.   (1180–2)

By this means he adjusts the critical balance of the poem, proving his own awareness of the objection which occurs to every reader of the Tale. When he wrote *The Clerk's Tale* Chaucer found no difficulty in reconciling its dream-like remoteness with his function as a courtly poet, whose work was expected to provide a vision of unearthly perfection. In his final work he discarded romantic illusion, turning with imaginative excitement to a world peopled by unambiguously actual housewives and artisans, and filled with the familiar appurtenances of everyday life—ladders and kneading-tubs, a widow's cabbage-patch, Sunday hats, a leather purse ornamented with metalwork. Set down in this context of realism, *The Clerk's Tale* might have appeared comically incongruous. Chaucer protects his story from ridicule by making the Clerk himself warn the pilgrims not to take it seriously, and by using it as a base from which he can satirize the Wife of Bath's impudence and immodesty.

Although the courtly tales which Chaucer brought into his collection are sometimes uneasily paired with their story-tellers, it is appropriate that *The Canterbury Tales* should include examples of his earlier writing. Whether this final work provides a panoramic survey of medieval life and character seems disputable, since Chaucer was above all a creative writer and not an historian of contemporary manners; but *The Canterbury Tales* certainly represents many aspects of his imaginative being. It is the world of himself, and not only of fourteenth-century England, that Chaucer's great poem displays with such unrestrained freedom. Within its accommodating design some earlier tales, written in a style which Chaucer had largely outgrown by the end of his career, find a fitting place. The poet presents himself in depth, and not at a single point of creative development. Moreover, it would be wrong to suppose that the work of Chaucer's final phase excludes awareness of the charmed circle into which the poet-dreamer had been led in many earlier poems. Within the enclosure of sticks surrounded by a ditch which characterizes unromantic reality, Chauntecleer and Pertelote may still discuss learned topics and make elegant conversation in true courtly manner. In the same oblivious fashion the ladylike Prioress practises points of social refinement, surrounded by pilgrims smelling of their trades and noisily ignorant of what constitutes good breeding. An old subject is changed by its new setting, becoming comic as Chaucer's perspective widens to reveal the commonplace behind the ideal, the pitched battles of actual married life beside the disembodied grace of Griselda's unchanging mildness.

Set against the flesh-and-blood actuality of Chaucer's pilgrims, a fairy-tale was bound to be sceptically received. The story is implausible partly because it fails to make Walter's behaviour accountable, but more because it denies Griselda even the rudimentary instinct to protect her children from violent death. To the extent that no woman could undergo such arbitrary trials in such quietness of spirit, *The Clerk's Tale* could be regarded as mere fantasy, whose action turns upon quirks of human impulse that remain unaccountable to the end. Its strength lies in its truth of feeling. In themselves the crucial happenings are not remotely credible, yet by investing Griselda with an almost luminous purity of emotion Chaucer makes the events live through the sense of compassion which they arouse. Perhaps no woman could express grief in such wanly haunting terms, but Chaucer asks to be judged against the standards of poetic creation, and not by comparison with the rougher truth of common reality. His tale does not attempt to justify itself by fidelity to everyday experience. It stands by virtue of what it creates: an impression of sad, tranquil beauty like an image reflected in dark water, with power to move the inward recesses of human feeling.

NOTE ON THE TEXT

The text which follows is based upon that of F. N. Robinson (*The Complete Works of Geoffrey Chaucer*, 2nd ed., 1957). The punctuation has been revised, with special reference to the exclamation marks. Spelling has been partly rationalized, by substituting *i* for *y* wherever the change aids the modern reader and does not affect the semantic value of the word. Thus *smylyng* becomes 'smiling', and *nyghtyngale* 'nightingale', but *wyn* (wine), *lyk* (like), and *fyr* (fire) are allowed to stand.

No accentuation has been provided in this text, for two reasons. First, because it produces a page displeasing to the eye; secondly, because it no longer seems necessary or entirely reliable in the light of modern scholarship. It is not now thought that the later works of Chaucer were written in a ten-syllable line from which no variation was permissible. The correct reading of a line of Chaucer is now seen to be more closely related to the correct reading of a comparable line of prose with phrasing suited to the rhythms of speech. This allows the reader to be more flexible in his interpretation of the line, and makes it unreasonably pedantic to provide a rigid system of accentuation.

NOTE ON PRONUNCIATION

These equivalences are intended to offer only a rough guide. For further detail, see *An Introduction to Chaucer*.

SHORT VOWELS

ă represents the sound now written *u*, as in 'cut'

ĕ as in modern 'set'

ĭ as in modern 'is'

ŏ as in modern 'top'

ŭ as in modern 'put' (not as in 'cut')

final -*e* represents the neutral vowel sound in '*a*bout' or 'atten*ti*on'. It is silent when the next word in the line begins with a vowel or an *h*.

Note on the Text

LONG VOWELS

ā as in modern 'car' (not as in 'name')

ē (open—i.e. where the equivalent modern word is spelt with *ea*) as in modern 'there'

ē (close—i.e. where the equivalent modern word is spelt with *ee* or *e*) represents the sound now written *a* as in 'take'

ī as in modern 'machine' (not as in 'like')

ō (open—i.e. where the equivalent modern vowel is pronounced as in 'br*o*ther', 'm*oo*d', or 'g*oo*d') represents the sound now written *aw* as in 'fawn'

ō (close—i.e. where the equivalent modern vowel is pronounced as in 'road') as in modern 'note'

ū as in French *tu* or German *Tür*

DIPHTHONGS

ai and *ei* both roughly represent the sound now written *i* or *y* as in 'die' or 'dye'

au and *aw* both represent the sound now written *ow* or *ou* as in 'now' or 'pounce'

ou and *ow* have two pronunciations: as in *through* where the equivalent modern vowel is pronounced as in 'through' or 'mouse'; and as in *pounce* where the equivalent modern vowel is pronounced as in 'know' or 'thought'

WRITING OF VOWELS AND DIPHTHONGS

A long vowel is often indicated by doubling, as in *roote* or *eek*. The *ŭ* sound is sometimes represented by an *o* as in *yong*. The *au* sound is sometimes represented by an *a*, especially before *m* or *n*, as in *cha(u)mbre* or *cha(u)nce*.

CONSONANTS

Largely as in modern English, except that many consonants now silent were still pronounced. *Gh* was pronounced as in Scottish 'lo*ch*', and both consonants should be pronounced in such groups as the following: '*gn*acchen', '*kn*ave', 'wor*d*', 'fol*k*', '*wr*ong'.

THE CLERK'S PROLOGUE

'Sire Clerk of Oxenford,' oure Hooste saide,
'Ye ride as coy and stille as dooth a maide
Were newe spoused, sittinge at the bord;
This day ne herde I of youre tonge a word.
I trowe ye studie aboute som sophime;   5
But Salomon seith "every thing hath time."

For Goddes sake, as beth of bettre cheere!
It is no time for to studien heere.
Telle us som myrie tale, by youre fey!
For what man that is entred in a pley,   10
He nedes moot unto the pley assente.
But precheth nat, as freres doon in Lente,
To make us for oure olde sinnes wepe,
Ne that thy tale make us nat to slepe.

Telle us som murie thing of aventures.   15
Youre termes, youre colours, and youre figures,
Keepe hem in stoor til so be that ye endite
Heigh style, as whan that men to kinges write.
Spekketh so pleyn at this time, we yow preye,
That we may understonde what ye seye.'   20
This worthy clerk benignely answerde:
'Hooste,' quod he, 'I am under youre yerde;
Ye han of us as now the governance,
And therfore wol I do yow obeisance,
As fer as resoun axeth, hardily.   25
I wol yow telle a tale which that I
Lerned at Padowe of a worthy clerk,
As preved by his wordes and his werk.
He is now deed and nailed in his cheste,

30   I prey to God so yeve his soule reste!
      Frounceys Petrak, the lauriat poete,
Highte this clerk, whos rethorike sweete
Enlumined al Itaille of poetrie,
As Linian dide of philosophie,
35   Or lawe, or oother art particuler;
But deeth, that wol nat suffre us dwellen heer,
But as it were a twinkling of an ye,
Hem bothe hath slain, and alle shul we die.
      But forth to tellen of this worthy man
40   That taughte me this tale, as I bigan,
I seye that first with heigh stile he enditeth,
Er he the body of his tale writeth,
A prohemie, in the which discriveth he
Pemond, and of Saluces the contree,
45   And speketh of Apennyn, the hilles hye,
That been the boundes of West Lumbardie,
And of Mount Vesulus in special,
Where as the Poo out of a welle smal
Taketh his firste springing and his sours,
50   That estward ay encresseth in his cours
To Emele-ward, to Ferrare, and Venise;
The which a long thing were to devise.
And trewely, as to my juggement,
Me thinketh it a thing impertinent,
55   Save that he wole conveyen his mateere;
But this his tale, which that ye may heere.'

THE CLERK'S TALE

Part I

Ther is, right at the west side of Itaille,
Doun at the roote of Vesulus the colde,
A lusty plain, habundant of vitaille,
Where many a tour and toun thou maist biholde, 60
That founded were in time of fadres olde,
And many another delitable sighte,
And Saluces this noble contree highte.

A markis whilom lord was of that lond,
As were his worthy eldres him bifore; 65
And obeisant, ay redy to his hond,
Were alle his liges, bothe lasse and moore.
Thus in delit he liveth, and hath doon yoore,
Biloved and drad, thurgh favour of Fortune,
Bothe of his lordes and of his commune. 70

Therwith he was, to speke as of linage,
The gentilleste yborn of Lumbardie,
A fair persone, and strong, and yong of age,
And ful of honour and of curteisie;
Discreet ynogh his contree for to gye, 75
Save in somme thinges that he was to blame;
And Walter was this yonge lordes name.

I blame him thus, that he considered noght
In time cominge what mighte him bitide,
But on his lust present was al his thoght, 80
As for to hauke and hunte on every side.
Wel ny alle othere cures leet he slide,
And eek he nolde—and that was worst of alle—
Wedde no wyf, for noght that may bifalle.

85   Oonly that point his peple bar so soore
That flokmeele on a day they to him wente,
And oon of hem, that wisest was of loore—
Or elles that the lord best wolde assente
That he sholde telle him what his peple mente,
90 Or elles koude he shewe wel swich mateere—
He to the markis seyde as ye shul heere:

    'O noble markis, youre humanitee
Asseureth us and yeveth us hardinesse,
As ofte as time is of necessitee,
95 That we to yow mowe telle oure hevinesse.
Accepteth, lord, now of youre gentillesse
That we with pitous herte unto yow pleyne,
And lat youre eres nat my vois desdeyne.

    'Al have I noght to doone in this mateere
100 Moore than another man hath in this place,
Yet for as muche as ye, my lord so deere,
Han alwey shewed me favour and grace
I dar the bettre aske of yow a space
Of audience, to shewen oure requeste,
105 And ye, my lord, to doon right as yow leste.

    'For certes, lord, so wel us liketh yow
And al youre werk, and evere han doon, that we
Ne koude nat us self devisen how
We mighte liven in moore felicitee,
110 Save o thing, lord, if it youre wille be,
That for to been a wedded man yow leste;
Thanne were youre peple in sovereyn hertes reste.

    'Boweth youre nekke under that blisful yok
Of soveraineetee, noght of servise,
115 Which that men clepe spousaille or wedlok;
And thenketh, lord, among youre thoghtes wise

How that oure dayes passe in sondry wise;
For thogh we slepe, or wake, or rome, or ride,
Ay fleeth the time; it nil no man abide.

   'And thogh youre grene youthe floure as yit,   120
In crepeth age alwey, as stille as stoon,
And deeth manaceth every age, and smyt
In ech estaat, for ther escapeth noon;
And al so certein as we knowe echoon
That we shul deye, as uncerteyn we alle   125
Been of that day whan deeth shal on us falle.

   'Accepteth thanne of us the trewe entente,
That nevere yet refuseden thyn heeste,
And we wol, lord, if that ye wole assente,
Chese yow a wyf, in short time atte leeste,   130
Born of the gentilleste and of the meeste
Of al this land, so that it oghte seme
Honour to God and yow, as we kan deeme.

   'Delivere us out of al this bisy drede,
And taak a wyf, for hye Goddes sake!   135
For if it so bifelle, as God forbede,
That thurgh youre deeth youre linage sholde slake,
And that a straunge successour sholde take
Youre heritage, O, wo were us alive!
Wherfore we pray you hastily to wive.'   140

   Hir meeke preyere and hir pitous cheere
Made the markis herte han pitee.
'Ye wol,' quod he, 'myn owene peple deere,
To that I nevere erst thoughte streyne me.
I me rejoised of my liberte,   145
That seelde time is founde in mariage;
Ther I was free, I moot been in servage.

   'But nathelees I se youre trewe entente,

And truste upon youre wit, and have doon ay;
150 Wherfore of my free wil I wole assente
To wedde me, as soone as evere I may.
But ther as ye han profred me to-day
To chese me a wyf, I yow relesse
That chois, and prey yow of that profre cesse.

155 'For God it woot, that children ofte been
Unlyk hir worthy eldres hem bifore;
Bountee comth al of God, nat of the streen
Of which they been engendred and ybore.
I truste in Goddes bountee, and therfore
160 My mariage and myn estaat and reste
I him bitake; he may doon as him leste.

'Lat me allone in chesinge of my wyf,—
That charge upon my bak I wole endure.
But I yow preye, and charge upon youre lyf,
165 That what wyf that I take, ye me assure
To worshipe hire, whil that hir lyf may dure,
In word and werk, bothe heere and everywheere,
As she an emperoures doghter weere.

'And forthermoore, this shal ye swere, that ye
170 Again my chois shul neither grucche ne strive;
For sith I shal forgoon my libertee
At youre requeste, as evere moot I thrive,
Ther as myn herte is set, ther wol I wive;
And but ye wole assente in swich manere,
175 I prey yow, speketh namoore of this matere.'

With hertely wil they sworen and assenten
To al this thing, ther seyde no wight nay;
Bisekinge him of grace, er that they wenten,
That he wolde graunten hem a certein day
180 Of his spousaille, as soone as evere he may;

For yet alwey the peple somwhat dredde,
Lest that the markis no wyf wolde wedde.

   He graunted hem a day, swich as him leste,
On which he wolde be wedded sikerly,
And seyde he dide al this at hir requeste.   185
And they, with humble entente, buxomly,
Knelinge upon hir knees ful reverently,
Him thonken alle; and thus they han an ende
Of hire entente, and hoom again they wende.

   And heerupon he to his officeres   190
Comaundeth for the feste to purveye,
And to his privee knightes and squieres
Swich charge yaf as him liste on hem leye;
And they to his comandement obeye,
And ech of hem dooth al his diligence   195
To doon unto the feeste reverence.

Part 2

   Noght fer fro thilke paleys honurable,
Wher as this markis shoop his mariage,
There stood a throop, of site delitable,
In which that povre folk of that village   200
Hadden hir beestes and hir herbergage,
And of hire labour tooke hir sustenance,
After that the erthe yaf hem habundance.

   Amonges thise povre folk ther dwelte a man
Which that was holden povrest of hem alle;   205
But hye God somtime senden kan
His grace into a litel oxes stalle;
Janicula men of that throop him calle.
A doghter hadde he, fair ynogh to sighte,
And Grisildis this yonge maiden highte.   210

But for to speke of vertuous beautee,
Thanne was she oon the faireste under sonne;
For povreliche yfostred up was she,
No likerous lust was thurgh hire herte yronne.
215 Wel ofter of the welle than of the tonne
She drank, and for she wolde vertu plese,
She knew wel labour, but noon idel ese.

But thogh this maide tendre were of age,
Yet in the brest of hire virginitee
220 Ther was enclosed ripe and sad corage;
And in greet reverence and charitee
Hir olde povre fader fostred shee.
A fewe sheep, spinninge, on feeld she kepte;
She wolde noght been idel til she slepte.

225 And whan she homward cam, she wolde bringe
Wortes or othere herbes times ofte,
The whiche she shredde and seeth for hir livinge,
And made hir bed ful hard and nothing softe;
And ay she kepte hir fadres lyf on-lofte
230 With everich obeisaunce and diligence
That child may doon to fadres reverence.

Upon Grisilde, this povre creature,
Ful ofte sithe this markis sette his ye
As he on hunting rood paraventure;
235 And whan it fil that he mighte hire espie,
He noght with wantown looking of folie
His eyen caste on hire, but in sad wise
Upon hir chiere he wolde him ofte avise,

Commendinge in his herte hir wommanhede,
240 And eek hir vertu, passinge any wight
Of so yong age, as wel in chiere as dede.
For thogh the peple have no greet insight

In vertu, he considered ful right
Hir bountee, and disposed that he wolde
Wedde hire oonly, if evere he wedde sholde.   245

   The day of wedding cam, but no wight kan
Telle what womman that it sholde be;
For which merveille wondred many a man,
And seyden, whan they were in privetee,
'Wol nat oure lord yet leve his vanitee?   250
Wol he nat wedde? allas; allas, the while!
Why wole he thus himself and us bigile?'

   But nathelees this markis hath doon make
Of gemmes, set in gold and in asure,
Brooches and ringes, for Grisildis sake;   255
And of hir clothing took he the mesure
By a maide lyk to hire stature,
And eek of othere aornementes alle
That unto swich a wedding sholde falle.

   The time of undren of the same day   260
Approcheth, that this wedding sholde be;
And al the paleys put was in array,
Bothe halle and chambres, ech in his degree;
Houses of office stuffed with plentee
Ther maistow seen, of deyntevous vitaille   265
That may be founde as fer as last Itaille.

   This roial markis, richely arrayed,
Lordes and ladies in his compaignie,
The whiche that to the feeste weren yprayed,
And of his retenue the bachelrie,   270
With many a soun of sondry melodie,
Unto the village of the which I tolde,
In this array the righte wey han holde.

   Grisilde of this, God woot, ful innocent,

275 That for hire shapen was al this array,
To fecchen water at a welle is went,
And cometh hoom as soone as ever she may;
For wel she hadde herd seyd that thilke day
The markis sholde wedde, and if she mighte,
280 She wolde fain han seyn som of that sighte.

She thoghte, 'I wole with othere maidens stonde,
That been my felawes, in oure dore and se
The markisesse, and therfore wol I fonde
To doon at hoom, as soone as it may be,
285 The labour which that longeth unto me;
And thanne I may at leyser hire biholde,
If she this wey unto the castel holde.'

And as she wolde over hir thresshfold gon,
The markis cam, and gan hire for to calle;
290 And she set doun hir water pot anon,
Biside the thresshfold, in an oxes stalle,
And doun upon hir knes she gan to falle,
And with sad contenance kneleth stille,
Til she had herd what was the lordes wille.

295 This thoghtful markis spak unto this maide
Ful sobrely, and seyde in this manere:
'Where is youre fader, O Grisildis?' he saide.
And she with reverence, in humble cheere,
Answerde, 'Lord, he is al redy heere.'
300 And in she gooth withouten lenger lette,
And to the markis she hir fader fette.

He by the hand thanne took this olde man,
And seyde thus, whan he him hadde aside:
'Janicula, I neither may ne kan
305 Lenger the plesance of myn herte hide.
If that thou vouche sauf, what so bitide,

Thy doghter wol I take, er that I wende,
As for my wyf, unto hir lives ende.

'Thou lovest me, I woot it wel certeyn,
And art my feithful lige man ybore;   310
And al that liketh me, I dar wel seyn
It liketh thee, and specially therfore
Tel me that point that I have seyd bifore,
If that thou wolt unto that purpos drawe,
To take me as for thy sone-in-lawe.'   315

This sodeyn cas this man astonied so
That reed he wax; abaist and al quakinge
He stood; unnethes seyde he wordes mo,
But oonly thus: 'Lord,' quod he, 'my willinge
Is as ye wole, ne ayeynes youre likinge   320
I wol no thing, ye be my lord so deere;
Right as yow lust, governeth this mateere.'

'Yet wol I,' quod this markis softely,
'That in thy chambre I and thou and she
Have a collacioun, and wostow why?   325
For I wol axe if it hire wille be
To be my wyf, and reule hire after me.
And al this shal be doon in thy presence;
I wol noght speke out of thyn audience.'

And in the chambre, whil they were aboute   330
Hir tretis, which as ye shal after heere,
The peple cam unto the hous withoute,
And wondred hem in how honest manere
And tentifly she kepte hir fader deere.
But outrely Grisildis wondre mighte,   335
For nevere erst ne saugh she swich a sighte.

No wonder is thogh that she were astoned
To seen so greet a gest come in that place;

She nevere was to swiche gestes woned,
340 For which she looked with ful pale face.
But shortly forth this matere for to chace,
Thise arn the wordes that the markis saide
To this benigne, verray, feithful maide.
  'Grisilde,' he seyde, 'ye shal wel understonde
345 It liketh to youre fader and to me
That I yow wedde, and eek it may so stonde,
As I suppose, ye wol that it so be.
But thise demandes axe I first,' quod he,
'That, sith it shal be doon in hastif wise,
350 Wol ye assente, or elles yow avise?
  'I seye this, be ye redy with good herte
To al my lust, and that I frely may,
As me best thinketh, do yow laughe or smerte,
And nevere ye to grucche it, night ne day?
355 And eek whan I sey "ye," ne sey nat "nay,"
Neither by word ne frowning contenance?
Swere this, and heere I swere oure alliance.'
  Wondringe upon this word, quakinge for drede,
She seyde, 'Lord, undigne and unworthy
360 Am I to thilke honour that ye me beede,
But as ye wole youreself, right so wol I.
And heere I swere that nevere willingly,
In werk ne thoght, I nil yow disobeye,
For to be deed, though me were looth to deye.'
365   'This is ynogh, Grisilde myn,' quod he.
And forth he gooth, with a ful sobre cheere,
Out at the dore, and after that cam she,
And to the peple he seyde in this manere:
'This is my wyf,' quod he, 'that standeth heere.
370 Honoureth hire and loveth hire, I preye,

Whoso me loveth; ther is namoore to seye.'
  And for that no thing of hir olde geere
She sholde bringe into his hous, he bad
That wommen sholde dispoillen hire right theere;
Of which thise ladies were nat right glad   375
To handle hir clothes, wherinne she was clad.
But nathelees, this maide bright of hewe
Fro foot to heed they clothed han al newe.

  Hir heris han they kembd, that lay untressed
Ful rudely, and with hir fingres smale   380
A corone on hire heed they han ydressed,
And sette hire ful of nowches grete and smale.
Of hire array what sholde I make a tale?
Unnethe the peple hir knew for hire fairnesse,
Whan she translated was in swich richesse.   385

  This markis hath hire spoused with a ring
Broght for the same cause, and thanne hire sette
Upon an hors, snow-whit and wel ambling,
And to his paleys, er he lenger lette,
With joyful peple that hire ladde and mette,   390
Conveyed hire, and thus the day they spende
In revel, til the sonne gan descende.

  And shortly forth this tale for to chace,
I seye that to this newe markisesse
God hath swich favour sent hire of his grace,   395
That it ne semed nat by liklinesse
That she was born and fed in rudenesse,
As in a cote or in an oxe-stalle,
But norissed in an emperoures halle.

  To every wight she woxen is so deere   400
And worshipful that folk ther she was bore,
And from hire birthe knewe hire yeer by yeere,

Unnethe trowed they,—but dorste han swore—
That to Janicle, of which I spak bifore,
405 She doghter were, for, as by conjecture,
Hem thoughte she was another creature.

For though that evere vertuous was she,
She was encressed in swich excellence
Of thewes goode, yset in heigh bountee,
410 And so discreet and fair of eloquence,
So benigne and so digne of reverence,
And koude so the peples herte embrace,
That ech hire lovede that looked in hir face.

Noght oonly of Saluces in the toun
415 Publiced was the bountee of hir name,
But eek biside in many a regioun,
If oon seyde wel, another seyde the same;
So spradde of hire heighe bountee the fame
That men and wommen, as wel yonge as olde,
420 Goon to Saluce, upon hire to biholde.

Thus Walter lowely—nay, but roially—
Wedded with fortunat honestetee,
In Goddes pees liveth ful esily
At hoom, and outward grace ynogh had he;
425 And for he saugh that under low degree
Was ofte vertu hid, the peple him heelde
A prudent man, and that is seyn ful seelde.

Nat oonly this Grisildis thurgh hir wit
Koude al the feet of wyfly hoomlinesse,
430 But eek, whan that the cas required it,
The commune profit koude she redresse.
Ther nas discord, rancour, ne hevinesse
In al that land, that she ne koude apese,
And wisely bringe hem alle in reste and ese.

Though that hire housbonde absent were anon,   435
If gentil men or othere of hire contree
Were wrothe, she wolde bringen hem aton;
So wise and ripe wordes hadde she,
And juggementz of so greet equitee,
That she from hevene sent was, as men wende,   440
Peple to save and every wrong t'amende.

Nat longe time after that this Grisild
Was wedded, she a doghter hath ybore.
Al had hire levere have born a knave child,
Glad was this markis and the folk therfore;   445
For though a maide child coome al bifore,
She may unto a knave child atteyne
By liklihede, sin she nis nat bareyne.

Part 3

Ther fil, as it bifalleth times mo,
Whan that this child had souked but a throwe,   450
This markis in his herte longeth so
To tempte his wyf, hir sadnesse for to knowe,
That he ne mighte out of his herte throwe
This merveillous desir his wyf t'assaye;
Nedelees, God woot, he thoghte hire for t'affraye.   455
He hadde assayed hire ynogh bifore,
And foond hire evere good; what neded it
Hire for to tempte, and alwey moore and moore,
Though som men preise it for a subtil wit?
But as for me, I seye that ivele it sit   460
To assaye a wyf whan that it is no nede,
And putten hire in angwissh and in drede.

For which this markis wroghte in this manere:
He cam allone a-night, ther as she lay,

465 With stierne face and with ful trouble cheere,
And seyde thus: 'Grisilde,' quod he, 'that day
That I yow took out of youre povere array,
And putte yow in estaat of heigh noblesse,—
Ye have nat that forgeten, as I gesse?

470 'I seye, Grisilde, this present dignitee,
In which that I have put yow, as I trowe,
Maketh yow nat foryetful for to be
That I yow took in povre estaat ful lowe,
For any wele ye moot youreselven knowe.

475 Taak heede of every word that I yow seye;
Ther is no wight that hereth it but we tweye.

'Ye woot youreself wel how that ye cam heere
Into this hous, it is nat longe ago;
And though to me that ye be lief and deere,

480 Unto my gentils ye be no thing so.
They seyn, to hem it is greet shame and wo
For to be subgetz and been in servage
To thee, that born art of a smal village.

'And namely sith thy doghter was ybore

485 Thise wordes han they spoken, doutelees.
But I desire, as I have doon bifore,
To live my lyf with hem in reste and pees.
I may nat in this caas be recchelees;
I moot doon with thy doghter for the beste,

490 Nat as I wolde, but as my peple leste.

'And yet, God woot, this is ful looth to me;
But nathelees withoute youre witing
I wol nat doon; but this wol I,' quod he,
'That ye to me assente as in this thing.

495 Shewe now youre pacience in youre werking,
That ye me highte and swore in youre village

That day that maked was oure mariage.'

Whan she had herd al this, she noght ameved
Neither in word, or chiere, or contenaunce;
For, as it semed, she was nat agreved.   500
She seyde, 'Lord, al lyth in youre plesaunce.
My child and I, with hertely obeisaunce,
Been youres al, and ye mowe save or spille
Youre owene thing; werketh after youre wille.

'Ther may no thing, God so my soule save,   505
Liken to yow that may displese me;
Ne I desire no thing for to have,
Ne drede for to leese, save oonly yee.
This wil is in myn herte, and ay shal be;
No lengthe of time or deeth may this deface,   510
Ne chaunge my corage to another place.'

Glad was this markis of hire answering,
But yet he feyned as he were nat so;
Al drery was his cheere and his looking,
Whan that he sholde out of the chambre go.   515
Soone after this, a furlong wey or two,
He prively hath toold al his entente
Unto a man, and to his wyf him sente.

A maner sergeant was this privee man,
The which that feithful ofte he founden hadde   520
In thinges grete, and eek swich folk wel kan
Doon execucioun in thinges badde.
The lord knew wel that he him loved and dradde;
And whan this sergeant wiste his lordes wille,
Into the chambre he stalked him ful stille.   525

'Madame,' he seyde, 'ye moote foryeve it me,
Though I do thing to which I am constreyned.
Ye been so wys that ful wel knowe ye

That lordes heestes mowe nat been yfeyned;
530 They mowe wel been biwailled or compleyned,
But men moote nede unto hire lust obeye,
And so wol I; ther is namoore to seye.

  'This child I am comanded for to take,'—
And spak namoore, but out the child he hente
535 Despitously, and gan a cheere make
As though he wolde han slain it er he wente.
Grisildis moot al suffre and al consente;
And as a lamb she sitteth meke and stille,
And leet this crueel sergeant doon his wille.

540   Suspecious was the diffame of this man,
Suspect his face, suspect his word also;
Suspect the time in which he this bigan.
Allas! hir doghter that she loved so,
She wende he wolde han slawen it right tho.
545 But nathelees she neither weep ne siked,
Conforminge hire to that the markis liked.

  But atte laste to speken she bigan,
And mekely she to the sergeant preyde,
So as he was a worthy gentil man,
550 That she moste kisse hire child er that it deyde.
And in hir barm this litel child she leyde
With ful sad face, and gan the child to blisse,
And lulled it, and after gan it kisse.

  And thus she seyde in hire benigne vois,
555 'Fareweel my child! I shal thee nevere see.
But sith I thee have marked with the crois
Of thilke Fader—blessed moote he be!—
That for us deyde upon a crois of tree,
Thy soule, litel child, I him bitake,
560 For this night shaltow dyen for my sake.'

I trowe that to a norice in this cas
It had been hard this reuthe for to se;
Wel mighte a mooder thanne han cryd 'allas!'
But nathelees so sad stidefast was she
That she endured al adversitee,   565
And to the sergeant mekely she saide,
'Have heer again youre litel yonge maide.

  'Gooth now,' quod she, 'and dooth my lordes
    heeste;
But o thing wol I prey yow of youre grace,
That, but my lord forbad yow, atte leeste   570
Burieth this litel body in som place
That beestes ne no briddes it torace.'
But he no word wol to that purpos seye,
But took the child and wente upon his weye.

  This sergeant cam unto his lord ageyn,   575
And of Grisildis wordes and hire cheere
He tolde him point for point, in short and pleyn,
And him presenteth with his doghter deere.
Somwhat this lord hadde routhe in his manere,
But nathelees his purpos heeld he stille,   580
As lordes doon, whan they wol han hir wille;

  And bad this sergeant that he prively
Sholde this child ful softe winde and wrappe,
With alle circumstances tendrely,
And carie it in a cofre or in a lappe;   585
But, upon peyne his heed of for to swappe,
That no man sholde knowe of his entente,
Ne whenne he cam, ne whider that he wente;

  But at Boloigne to his suster deere,
That thilke time of Panik was countesse,   590
He sholde it take, and shewe hire this mateere,

Bisekinge hire to doon hire bisinesse
This child to fostre in alle gentillesse;
And whos child that it was he bad hire hide
595 From every wight, for oght that may bitide.
  The sergeant gooth, and hath fulfild this thing;
But to this markis now retourne we.
For now gooth he ful faste imagining
If by his wives cheere he mighte se,
600 Or by hire word aperceive, that she
Were chaunged; but he nevere hire koude finde
But evere in oon ylike sad and kinde.
  As glad, as humble, as bisy in servise,
And eek in love, as she was wont to be,
605 Was she to him in every maner wise;
Ne of hir doghter noght a word spak she.
Noon accident, for noon adversitee,
Was seyn in hire, ne nevere hir doghter name
Ne nempned she, in ernest nor in game.

Part 4

610 In this estaat ther passed been foure yeer
Er she with childe was, but, as God wolde,
A knave child she bar by this Walter,
Ful gracious and fair for to biholde.
And whan that folk it to his fader tolde,
615 Nat oonly he, but al his contree merie
Was for this child, and God they thanke and herie.
  Whan it was two yeer old, and fro the brest
Departed of his norice, on a day
This markis caughte yet another lest
620 To tempte his wyf yet ofter, if he may.
O nedelees was she tempted in assay!

42

But wedded men ne knowe no mesure,
Whan that they finde a pacient creature.

   'Wyf,' quod this markis, 'ye han herd er this,
My peple sikly berth oure mariage;   625
And namely sith my sone yboren is,
Now is it worse than evere in al oure age.
The murmur sleeth myn herte and my corage,
For to mine eres comth the vois so smerte
That it wel ny destroyed hath myn herte.   630

   'Now sey they thus: "Whan Walter is agon,
Thanne shal the blood of Janicle succede
And been oure lord, for oother have we noon."
Swiche wordes seith my peple, out of drede.
Wel oughte I of swich murmur taken heede;   635
For certeinly I drede swich sentence,
Though they nat pleyn speke in myn audience.

   'I wolde live in pees, if that I mighte;
Wherfore I am disposed outrely,
As I his suster servede by nighte,   640
Right so thenke I to serve him prively.
This warne I yow, that ye nat sodeynly
Out of youreself for no wo sholde outreye;
Beth pacient, and therof I yow preye.'

   'I have,' quod she, 'seyd thus, and evere shal: 645
I wol no thing, ne nil no thing, certain,
But as yow list. Naught greveth me at al,
Though that my doughter and my sone be slain,—
At youre comandement, this is to sayn.
I have noght had no part of children tweyne 650
But first siknesse, and after, wo and peyne.

   'Ye been oure lord, dooth with youre owene thing
Right as yow list; axeth no reed at me.

43

For as I lefte at hoom al my clothing,
655   Whan I first cam to yow, right so,' quod she,
'Lefte I my wil and al my libertee,
And took youre clothing; wherfore I yow preye,
Dooth youre plesaunce, I wol youre lust obeye.
    'And certes, if I hadde prescience
660   Youre wil to knowe, er ye youre lust me tolde,
I wolde it doon withouten necligence;
But now I woot youre lust, and what ye wolde,
Al youre plesance ferme and stable I holde;
For wiste I that my deeth wolde do yow ese,
665   Right gladly wolde I dyen, yow to plese.
    'Deth may noght make no comparisoun
Unto youre love.' And whan this markis say
The constance of his wyf, he caste adoun
His eyen two, and wondreth that she may
670   In pacience suffre al this array;
And forth he goth with drery contenance,
But to his herte it was ful greet plesance.
    This ugly sergeant, in the same wise
That he hire doghter caughte, right so he,
675   Or worse, if men worse kan devise,
Hath hent hire sone, that ful was of beautee.
And evere in oon so pacient was she
That she no chiere maade of hevinesse,
But kiste hir sone, and after gan it blesse;
680   Save this, she preyede him that, if he mighte,
Hir litel sone he wolde in erthe grave,
His tendre limes, delicaat to sighte,
Fro foweles and fro beestes for to save.
But she noon answere of him mighte have.
685   He wente his wey, as him no thing ne roghte;

But to Boloigne he tendrely it broghte.
  This markis wondred, evere lenger the moore,
Upon hir pacience, and if that he
Ne hadde soothly knowen therbifoore
That parfitly hir children loved she,   690
He wolde have wend that of som subtiltee,
And of malice, or for crueel corage,
That she hadde suffred this with sad visage.
  But wel he knew that next himself, certain,
She loved hir children best in every wise.   695
But now of wommen wolde I axen fain
If thise assayes mighte nat suffise?
What koude a sturdy housbonde moore devise
To preeve hir wyfhod and hir stedefastnesse,
And he continuinge evere in sturdinesse?   700
  But ther been folk of swich condicion
That whan they have a certein purpos take,
They kan nat stinte of hire entencion,
But, right as they were bounden to a stake,
They wol nat of that firste purpos slake.   705
Right so this markis fulliche hath purposed
To tempte his wyf as he was first disposed.
  He waiteth if by word or contenance
That she to him was changed of corage;
But nevere koude he finde variance.   710
She was ay oon in herte and in visage;
And ay the forther that she was in age,
The moore trewe, if that it were possible,
She was to him in love, and moore penible.
  For which it semed thus, that of hem two   715
Ther nas but o wil; for, as Walter leste,
The same lust was hire plesance also.

And, God be thanked, al fil for the beste.
She shewed wel, for no worldly unreste
720 A wyf, as of hirself, nothing ne sholde
Wille in effect, but as hir housbonde wolde.
     The sclaundre of Walter ofte and wide spradde,
That of a crueel herte he wikkedly,
For he a povre womman wedded hadde,
725 Hath mordred bothe his children prively.
Swich murmur was among hem comunly.
No wonder is, for to the peples ere
Ther cam no word, but that they mordred were.
     For which, where as his peple therbifore
730 Hadde loved him wel, the sclaundre of his diffame
Made hem that they him hatede therfore.
To been a mordrere is an hateful name;
But nathelees, for ernest ne for game,
He of his crueel purpos nolde stente;
735 To tempte his wyf was set al his entente.
     Whan that his doghter twelve yeer was of age,
He to the court of Rome, in subtil wise
Enformed of his wil, sente his message,
Comaundinge hem swiche bulles to devise
740 As to his crueel purpos may suffise,
How that the pope, as for his peples reste,
Bad him to wedde another, if him leste.
     I seye, he bad they sholde countrefete
The popes bulles, makinge mencion
745 That he hath leve his firste wyf to lete,
As by the popes dispensacion,
To stinte rancour and dissencion
Bitwixe his peple and him; thus seyde the bulle,
The which they han publiced atte fulle.

46

The rude peple, as it no wonder is,   750
Wenden ful wel that it hadde be right so;
But whan thise tidinges came to Grisildis,
I deeme that hire herte was ful wo.
But she, ylike sad for everemo,
Disposed was, this humble creature,   755
The adversitee of Fortune al t'endure,
   Abidinge evere his lust and his plesance,
To whom that she was yeven herte and al,
As to hire verray worldly suffisance.
But shortly if this storie I tellen shal,   760
This markis writen hath in special
A lettre, in which he sheweth his entente,
And secreely he to Boloigne it sente.
   To the Erl of Panik, which that hadde tho
Wedded his suster, preyde he specially   765
To bringen hoom again his children two
In honurable estaat al openly.
But o thing he him preyede outrely,
That he to no wight, though men wolde enquere,
Sholde nat telle whos children that they were,   770
   But seye, the maiden sholde ywedded be
Unto the Markis of Saluce anon.
And as this erl was preyed, so dide he;
For at day set he on his wey is goon
Toward Saluce, and lordes many oon   775
In riche array, this maiden for to gide,
Hir yonge brother ridinge hire biside.
   Arrayed was toward hir mariage
This fresshe maide, ful of gemmes cleere;
Hir brother, which that seven yeer was of age,   780
Arrayed eek ful fressh in his manere.

47

And thus in greet noblesse and with glad cheere,
Toward Saluces shapinge hir journey,
Fro day to day they riden in hir wey.

Part 5

785 Among al this, after his wikke usage,
This markis, yet his wyf to tempte moore
To the outtreste preeve of hir corage,
Fully to han experience and loore
If that she were as stidefast as bifoore,
790 He on a day, in open audience,
Ful boistously hath seyd hire this sentence:
    'Certes, Grisilde, I hadde ynogh plesance
To han yow to my wyf for youre goodnesse,
As for youre trouthe and for youre obeisance,
795 Noght for youre linage, ne for youre richesse;
But now knowe I in verray soothfastnesse
That in greet lordshipe, if I wel avise,
Ther is greet servitute in sondry wise.
    'I may nat doon as every plowman may.
800 My peple me constreyneth for to take
Another wyf, and crien day by day;
And eek the pope, rancour for to slake,
Consenteth it, that dar I undertake;
And trewely thus muche I wol yow seye,
805 My newe wyf is cominge by the weye.
    'Be strong of herte, and voide anon hir place,
And thilke dowere that ye broghten me,
Taak it again; I graunte it of my grace.
Retourneth to youre fadres hous,' quod he;
810 'No man may alwey han prosperitee.
With evene herte I rede yow t'endure

The strook of Fortune or of aventure.'
   And she again answerde in pacience,
'My lord,' quod she, 'I woot, and wiste alway,
How that bitwixen youre magnificence   815
And my poverte no wight kan ne may
Maken comparison; it is no nay.
I ne heeld me nevere digne in no manere
To be youre wyf, no, ne youre chamberere.

   'And in this hous, ther ye me lady maade—   820
The heighe God take I for my witnesse,
And also wysly he my soule glaade—
I nevere heeld me lady ne mistresse,
But humble servant to youre worthinesse,
And evere shal, whil that my lyf may dure,   825
Aboven every worldly creature.

   'That ye so longe of youre benignitee
Han holden me in honour and nobleye,
Where as I was noght worthy for to bee,
That thonke I God and yow, to whom I preye   830
Foryelde it yow; ther is namoore to seye.
Unto my fader gladly wol I wende,
And with him dwelle unto my lives ende.

   'Ther I was fostred of a child ful smal,
Til I be deed my lyf ther wol I lede,   835
A widwe clene in body, herte, and al.
For sith I yaf to yow my maidenhede,
And am youre trewe wyf, it is no drede,
God shilde swich a lordes wyf to take
Another man to housbonde or to make!   840

   'And of youre newe wyf God of his grace
So graunte yow wele and prosperitee!
For I wol gladly yelden hire my place,

In which that I was blisful wont to bee.
845 For sith it liketh yow, my lord,' quod shee,
'That whilom weren al myn hertes reste,
That I shal goon, I wol goon whan yow leste.

'But ther as ye me profre swich dowaire
As I first broghte, it is wel in my minde
850 It were my wrecched clothes, nothing faire,
The whiche to me were hard now for to finde.
O goode God! how gentil and how kinde
Ye semed by youre speche and youre visage
The day that maked was oure mariage!

855 'But sooth is seyd—algate I finde it trewe,
For in effect it preeved is on me—
Love is noght oold as whan that it is newe.
But certes, lord, for noon adversitee,
To dyen in the cas, it shal nat bee
860 That evere in word or werk I shal repente
That I yow yaf myn herte in hool entente.

'My lord, ye woot that in my fadres place
Ye dide me streepe out of my povre weede,
And richely me cladden, of youre grace.
865 To yow broghte I noght elles, out of drede,
But feith, and nakednesse, and maidenhede;
And heere again your clothing I restoore,
And eek your wedding ring, for everemore.

'The remenant of youre jueles redy be
870 Inwith youre chambre, dar I saufly sayn.
Naked out of my fadres hous,' quod she,
'I cam, and naked moot I turne again.
Al youre plesance wol I folwen fain;
But yet I hope it be nat youre entente
875 That I smoklees out of youre paleys wente.

'Ye koude nat doon so dishonest a thing,
That thilke wombe in which youre children leye
Sholde biforn the peple, in my walking,
Be seyn al bare; wherfore I yow preye,
Lat me nat lyk a worm go by the weye.   880
Remembre yow, myn owene lord so deere,
I was youre wyf, though I unworthy weere.

'Wherfore, in gerdon of my maidenhede,
Which that I broghte, and noght again I bere,
As voucheth sauf to yeve me, to my meede,   885
But swich a smok as I was wont to were,
That I therwith may wrye the wombe of here
That was youre wyf. And heer take I my leeve
Of yow, myn owene lord, lest I yow greve.'

'The smok,' quod he, 'that thou hast on thy bak,   890
Lat it be stille, and bere it forth with thee.'
But wel unnethes thilke word he spak,
But wente his wey, for routhe and for pitee.
Biforn the folk hirselven strepeth she,
And in hir smok, with heed and foot al bare,   895
Toward hir fadre hous forth is she fare.

The folk hire folwe, wepinge in hir weye,
And Fortune ay they cursen as they goon;
But she fro weping kepte hire eyen dreye,
Ne in this time word ne spak she noon.   900
Hir fader, that this tidinge herde anoon,
Curseth the day and time that Nature
Shoop him to been a lives creature.

For out of doute this olde poure man
Was evere in suspect of hir mariage;   905
For evere he demed, sith that it bigan,
That whan the lord fulfild hadde his corage,

Him wolde thinke it were a disparage
To his estaat so lowe for t'alighte,
910   And voiden hire as soone as ever he mighte.
    Agains his doghter hastily goth he,
For he by noise of folk knew hire cominge,
And with hire olde coote, as it mighte be
He covered hire, ful sorwefully wepinge.
915   But on hire body mighte he it nat bringe,
For rude was the clooth, and moore of age
By dayes fele than at hire mariage.
    Thus with hire fader, for a certeyn space,
Dwelleth this flour of wyfly pacience,
920   That neither by hire wordes ne hire face,
Biforn the folk, ne eek in hire absence,
Ne shewed she that hire was doon offence;
Ne of hire heighe estaat no remembraunce
Ne hadde she, as by hire contenaunce.
925   No wonder is, for in hire grete estaat
Hire goost was evere in pleyn humilitee;
No tendre mouth, noon herte delicaat,
No pompe, no semblant of roialtee,
But ful of pacient beningnitee,
930   Discreet and pridelees, ay honurable,
And to hire housbonde evere meke and stable.
    Men speke of Job, and moost for his humblesse,
As clerkes, whan hem list, konne wel endite,
Namely of men, but as in soothfastnesse,
935   Though clerkes preise wommen but a lite,
Ther kan no man in humblesse him acquite
As womman kan, ne kan been half so trewe
As wommen been, but it be falle of newe.

Part 6

Fro Boloigne is this Erl of Panik come,
Of which the fame up sprang to moore and lesse, 940
And to the peples eres, alle and some,
Was kouth eek that a newe markisesse
He with him broghte, in swich pompe and richesse
That nevere was ther seyn with mannes ye
So noble array in al West Lumbardie. 945

The markis, which that shoop and knew al this,
Er that this erl was come, sente his message
For thilke sely povre Grisildis;
And she with humble herte and glad visage,
Nat with no swollen thoght in hire corage, 950
Cam at his heste, and on hire knees hire sette,
And reverently and wisely she him grette.

'Grisilde,' quod he, 'my wil is outrely,
This maiden, that shal wedded been to me,
Received be to-morwe as roially 955
As it possible is in myn hous to be,
And eek that every wight in his degree
Have his estaat, in sitting and servise
And heigh plesaunce, as I kan best devise.

'I have no wommen suffisaunt, certain, 960
The chambres for t'arraye in ordinaunce
After my lust, and therfore wolde I fain
That thyn were al swich manere governaunce.
Thou knowest eek of old al my plesaunce;
Thogh thyn array be badde and ivel biseye, 965
Do thou thy devoir at the leeste weye.'

'Nat oonly, lord, that I am glad,' quod she,
'To doon youre lust, but I desire also

53

Yow for to serve and plese in my degree
970 Withouten feynting, and shal everemo;
Ne nevere, for no wele ne no wo,
Ne shal the goost withinne myn herte stente
To love yow best with al my trewe entente.'

And with that word she gan the hous to dighte,
975 And tables for to sette, and beddes make;
And peyned hire to doon al that she mighte,
Preyinge the chambereres, for Goddes sake,
To hasten hem, and faste swepe and shake;
And she, the mooste servisable of alle,
980 Hath every chambre arrayed and his halle.

Abouten undren gan this erl alighte,
That with him broghte thise noble children tweye,
For which the peple ran to seen the sighte
Of hire array, so richely biseye;
985 And thanne at erst amonges hem they seye
That Walter was no fool, thogh that him leste
To chaunge his wyf, for it was for the beste.

For she is fairer, as they deemen alle,
Than is Grisilde, and moore tendre of age,
990 And fairer fruit bitwene hem sholde falle,
And moore plesant, for hire heigh linage.
Hir brother eek so fair was of visage
That hem to seen the peple hath caught plesaunce,
Commendinge now the markis governaunce.—

995 'O stormy peple! unsad and evere untrewe!
Ay undiscreet and chaunginge as a fane!
Delitinge evere in rumbul that is newe,
For lyk the moone ay wexe ye and wane!
Ay ful of clapping, deere ynogh a jane!
1000 Youre doom is fals, youre constance ivele preeveth;

A ful greet fool is he that on yow leeveth.'
   Thus seyden sadde folk in that citee,
Whan that the peple gazed up and doun;
For they were glad, right for the noveltee,
To han a newe lady of hir toun.   1005
Namoore of this make I now mencioun,
But to Grisilde again wol I me dresse,
And telle hir constance and hir bisinesse.—
   Ful bisy was Grisilde in every thing
That to the feeste was apertinent.   1010
Right noght was she abaist of hire clothing,
Thogh it were rude and somdeel eek torent;
But with glad cheere to the yate is went
With oother folk, to greete the markisesse,
And after that dooth forth hire bisinesse.   1015
   With so glad chiere his gestes she receiveth,
And konningly, everich in his degree,
That no defaute no man aperceiveth,
But ay they wondren what she mighte bee
That in so povre array was for to see,   1020
And koude swich honour and reverence,
And worthily they preisen hire prudence.
   In al this meene while she ne stente
This maide and eek hir brother to commende
With al hir herte, in ful beningne entente,   1025
So wel that no man koude hir pris amende.
But atte laste, whan that thise lordes wende
To sitten doun to mete, he gan to calle
Grisilde, as she was bisy in his halle.
   'Grisilde,' quod he, as it were in his pley,   1030
'How liketh thee my wyf and hire beautee?'
'Right wel,' quod she, 'my lord; for, in good fey,

A fairer saugh I nevere noon than she.
I prey to God yeve hire prosperitee;
And so hope I that he wol to yow sende
Plesance ynogh unto youre lives ende.

   'O thing biseke I yow, and warne also,
That ye ne prikke with no tormentinge
This tendre maiden, as ye han doon mo;
For she is fostred in hire norissinge
Moore tendrely, and, to my supposinge,
She koude nat adversitee endure
As koude a povre fostred creature.'

   And whan this Walter saugh hire pacience,
Hir glade chiere, and no malice at al,
And he so ofte had doon to hire offence,
And she ay sad and constant as a wal,
Continuinge evere hire innocence overal,
This sturdy markis gan his herte dresse
To rewen upon hire wyfly stedfastnesse.

   'This is ynogh, Grisilde myn,' quod he;
'Be now namoore agast ne ivele apayed.
I have thy feith and thy beningnitee,
As wel as evere womman was, assayed,
In greet estaat, and povreliche arrayed.
Now knowe I, dere wyf, thy stedfastnesse,'—
And hire in armes took and gan hire kesse.

   And she for wonder took of it no keep;
She herde nat what thing he to hire seyde;
She ferde as she had stert out of a sleep,
Til she out of hire mazednesse abreyde.
'Grisilde,' quod he, 'by God, that for us deyde,
Thou art my wyf, ne noon oother I have,
Ne nevere hadde, as God my soule save!

1035
1040
1045
1050
1055
1060

'This is thy doghter, which thou hast supposed 1065
To be my wyf; that oother feithfully
Shal be myn heir, as I have ay disposed;
Thou bare him in thy body trewely.
At Boloigne have I kept hem prively;
Taak hem again, for now maistow nat seye 1070
That thou hast lorn noon of thy children tweye.

'And folk that ootherweys han seyd of me,
I warne hem wel that I have doon this deede
For no malice, ne for no crueltee,
But for t'assaye in thee thy wommanheede, 1075
And nat to sleen my children—God forbeede!
But for to kepe hem prively and stille,
Til I thy purpos knewe and al thy wille.'

Whan she this herde, aswowne doun she falleth
For pitous joye, and after hire swowninge 1080
She bothe hire yonge children to hire calleth,
And in hire armes, pitously wepinge,
Embraceth hem, and tendrely kissinge
Ful lyk a mooder, with hire salte teeres
She bathed bothe hire visage and hire heeres. 1085

O which a pitous thing it was to se
Hir swowning, and hire humble vois to heere!
'Grauntmercy, lord, God thanke it yow,' quod she,
'That ye han saved me my children deere!
Now rekke I nevere to been deed right heere; 1090
Sith I stonde in youre love and in youre grace,
No fors of deeth, ne whan my spirit pace!

'O tendre, o deere, o yonge children mine!
Youre woful mooder wende stedfastly
That crueel houndes or som foul vermine 1095
Hadde eten yow; but God, of his mercy,

57

And youre beningne fader tendrely
Hath doon yow kept,'—and in that same stounde
Al sodeynly she swapte adoun to grounde.

1100   And in hire swough so sadly holdeth she
Hire children two, whan she gan hem t'embrace,
That with greet sleighte and greet difficultee
The children from hire arm they gonne arace.
O many a teere on many a pitous face
1105 Doun ran of hem that stooden hire biside;
Unnethe abouten hire mighte they abide.

    Walter hire gladeth, and hire sorwe slaketh;
She riseth up, abaised, from hire traunce,
And every wight hire joye and feeste maketh
1110 Til she hath caught again hire contenaunce.
Walter hire dooth so feithfully plesaunce
That it was deyntee for to seen the cheere
Bitwixe hem two, now they been met yfeere.

    Thise ladies, whan that they hir time say,
1115 Han taken hire and into chambre gon,
And strepen hire out of hire rude array,
And in a clooth of gold that brighte shoon,
With a coroune of many a riche stoon
Upon hire heed, they into halle hire broghte,
1120 And ther she was honured as hire oghte.

    Thus hath this pitous day a blisful ende,
For every man and womman dooth his might
This day in murthe and revel to dispende
Til on the welkne shoon the sterres light.
1125 For moore solempne in every mannes sight
This feste was, and gretter of costage,
Than was the revel of hire mariage.

    Ful many a yeer in heigh prosperitee

Liven thise two in concord and in reste,
And richely his doghter maried he   1130
Unto a lord, oon of the worthieste
Of al Itaille; and thanne in pees and reste
His wives fader in his court he kepeth,
Til that the soule out of his body crepeth.

   His sone succedeth in his heritage   1135
In reste and pees, after his fader day,
And fortunat was eek in mariage,
Al putte he nat his wyf in greet assay.
This world is nat so strong, it is no nay,
As it hath been in olde times yoore,   1140
And herkneth what this auctour seith therfoore.

   This storie is seyd, nat for that wives sholde
Folwen Grisilde as in humilitee,
For it were inportable, though they wolde;
But for that every wight, in his degree,   1145
Sholde be constant in adversitee
As was Grisilde; therfore Petrak writeth
This storie, which with heigh stile he enditeth.

   For, sith a womman was so pacient
Unto a mortal man, wel moore us oghte   1150
Receiven al in gree that God us sent;
For greet skile is, he preeve that he wroghte.
But he ne tempteth no man that he boghte,
As seith Seint Jame, if ye his pistel rede;
He preeveth folk al day, it is no drede,   1155

   And suffreth us, as for oure excercise,
With sharpe scourges of adversitee
Ful ofte to be bete in sondry wise;
Nat for to knowe oure wil, for certes he,
Er we were born, knew al oure freletee;   1160

59

And for oure beste is al his governaunce.
Lat us thanne live in vertuous suffraunce.
    But o word, lordinges, herkneth er I go:
It were ful hard to finde now-a-dayes
In al a toun Grisildis thre or two;
For if that they were put to swiche assayes,
The gold of hem hath now so badde alayes
With bras, that thogh the coine be fair at ye,
It wolde rather breste a-two than plie.
    For which heere, for the Wives love of Bathe—
Whos lyf and al hire secte God maintene
In heigh maistrie, and elles were it scathe—
I wol with lusty herte, fressh and grene,
Seyn yow a song to glade yow, I wene;
And lat us stinte of ernestful matere.
Herkneth my song that seith in this manere:
    Grisilde is deed, and eek hire pacience,
And bothe atones buried in Itaille;
For which I crie in open audience,
No wedded man so hardy be t'assaille
His wives pacience in trust to finde
Grisildis, for in certein he shal faille.
    O noble wives, ful of heigh prudence,
Lat noon humilitee youre tonge naille,
Ne lat no clerk have cause or diligence
To write of yow a storie of swich mervaille
As of Grisildis pacient and kinde,
Lest Chichevache yow swelwe in hire entraille!
    Folweth Ekko, that holdeth no silence,
But evere answereth at the countretaille.
Beth nat bidaffed for youre innocence,
But sharply taak on yow the governaille.

1165
1170
1175
1180
1185
1190

Emprenteth wel this lessoun in youre minde,
For commune profit sith it may availle.

    Ye archewives, stondeth at defense,   1195
Sin ye be strong as is a greet camaille;
Ne suffreth nat that men yow doon offense.
And sklendre wives, fieble as in bataille,
Beth egre as is a tigre yond in Inde;
Ay clappeth as a mille, I yow consaille.   1200
  Ne dreed hem nat, doth hem no reverence,
For though thyn housbonde armed be in maille,
The arwes of thy crabbed eloquence
Shal perce his brest, and eek his aventaille.
In jalousie I rede eek thou him binde,   1205
And thou shalt make him couche as doth a quaille.

    If thou be fair, ther folk been in presence,
Shewe thou thy visage and thyn apparaille;
If thou be foul, be fre of thy dispence;
To gete thee freendes ay do thy travaille;   1210
Be ay of chiere as light as leef on linde,
And lat him care, and wepe, and wringe, and waille!

NOTES

The following abbreviations have been used in the notes:

French   *A Chaucer Handbook*, by R. D. French. 2nd ed., New York, 1947

LG   *Le Livre Griseldis*, transcribed by J. B. Severs and printed in *The Literary Relationships of Chaucer's Clerkes Tale*. London, 1942

ME   Middle English

OE   Old English

Petrarch   *Epistolae Seniles*, XVII, 3; reprinted in *The Literary Relationships of Chaucer's Clerkes Tale*, by J. B. Severs

Robinson   *The Complete Works of Geoffrey Chaucer*, ed. F. N. Robinson. 2nd ed., Oxford, 1957

Sisam   *The Clerk's Tale*, ed. K. Sisam. Oxford, 1961

1. *Sire Clerk of Oxenford* For Chaucer's description of the Clerk, a scholar at Oxford, see the *General Prologue*, lines 287–310. The Host has previously addressed this pilgrim as 'sire Clerk' in line 842 of the same work. So used, the prefix has the same sense as modern 'mister': compare 'sire Monk' and 'sir John' in the Prologue to *The Nun's Priest's Tale*.

2. *coy and stille* 'reserved and quiet'; conforming with the portrait in the *General Prologue*.

3. *were newe spoused* 'newly married'.
   the bord 'the table at the wedding-feast'.

5. *som sophime* 'some sophism or other'; a subtle intellectual argument. The Host mocks the Clerk's withdrawn manner at the end of the *General Prologue*, lines 842–3: 'Lat be youre shamefastnesse, Ne studieth noght!'

6. *Salomon* Solomon (see Ecclesiastes iii. 1).

7. *Goddes* 'God's'. For similar genitive forms see line 231 below, *fadres*, father's; line 294, *lordes*, lord's; line 1133, *wives*, wife's.
   as beth 'be'. The pleonastic use of *as* before imperatives is common in Chaucer: cp. line 885 below, 'as voucheth sauf'.

10. *what man that is entred in a pley* 'a man who joins in a game'.

62

11. *unto the pley assente* 'abide by the rules'.

12. *precheth* 'preach'; the polite imperative form.

14. *ne that thy tale make us nat to slepe* 'see that your tale doesn't send us to sleep'. Double negatives are accepted in ME grammar. At their setting-out, the pilgrims have been warned to make their tales satisfy two criteria, 'best sentence and moost solaas', to be edifying and entertaining. The Host fears that the Clerk may be too intent upon instruction.

15. *som murie thing* 'some cheerful tale'. For 'thing' in the sense of a short story see *The Wife of Bath's Tale*, line 952, where the speaker refers to Ovid's *Metamorphoses* as 'thinges smale'.

16. *youre termes, youre colours, and youre figures* 'your various rhetorical devices'. *Termes* are technical expressions, *colours* are figures of speech, and *figures* are ornamental literary forms such as hyperbole and metaphor. For a detailed account of medieval rhetoric, see *An Introduction to Chaucer*, ch. 4, and *The Franklin's Tale*, ed. Phyllis Hodgson, London, 1960, pp. 73–6.

17. *til so be that ye endite* 'until such time as you compose'.

18. *heigh style* The phrase rests upon a misreading of Petrarch —see note on line 1141 below—but Chaucer's intentions are clear. The Host's repudiation of a dignified courtly style in favour of plain colloquial English may have some significance for the change which Chaucer's own style underwent between his composing the Tale and the Prologue.

22. *under youre yerde* In common with the other pilgrims, the Clerk has submitted himself to the Host's authority before setting out from London, when the company accepts his terms; 'alle by oon assent For to stonden at my juggement'.

23. *as now* 'for this time'.

24. *wol I do yow obeisance* 'I will obey you'.

25. *as fer as resoun axeth, hardily* 'within all reasonable limits, without question'.

27. *Padowe* Padua, seat of one of the famous medieval universities. It was common for medieval scholars to move about Europe, studying at a number of different universities.

a worthy clerk We should describe Petrarch as a poet rather than as a scholar, but as one of the earliest humanists, deeply read in classical literature, he certainly deserves this attractive title.

31. *Frounceys Petrak* Francesco Petrarca, or Petrarch, 1304–74.

He is best remembered today for the long sequence of love-poems, addressed to Laura, whose literary influence continued into the seventeenth century.

lauriat poete Petrarch was crowned poet laureate at Rome in 1341.

32. *highte this clerk* The order of the sentence is 'This scholar was called Francesco Petrarca . . .'.

whos rethorike sweete 'whose eloquence as a writer'.

33. *enlumined al Itaille of poetrie* 'gave lustre to Italian poetry generally'.

34. *Linian* Giovanni da Lignaco, professor of Canon Law at Bologna during the fourteenth century.

philosophie Probably natural philosophy. Lignaco also wrote on law, ethics, theology and astronomy.

38. *alle shul we die* 'all of us will die'. Cp. the passage on death, derived from Petrarch's version of the tale, in lines 121–3 below.

41. *first with heigh stile he enditeth* Petrarch introduces his tale with a dignified description of its setting, much longer than the brief reference given in lines 57–63 of *The Clerk's Tale*. When he wrote the Prologue, Chaucer repeated and extended this description, adding many of the details from Petrarch which are omitted in the opening stanza of the Tale, but without attempting to imitate Petrarch's lofty style. The rhyme-royal of the Tale might be regarded as the more dignified style which Chaucer had now rejected in favour of decasyllabic couplets.

44. *Pemond* Piedmont.

Saluces Saluzzo, a marquisate with a capital town of the same name, about forty miles west of Turin.

47. *Mount Vesulus* Monte Viso, now on the frontier between Italy and France.

48. *where as* 'where'.

51. *to Emele-ward, to Ferrare, and Venise* 'towards the provinces of Emilia and Ferrara, and the state of Venice'.

54. *me thinketh it a thing impertinent* 'it seems to me an irrelevant matter'. Coming after the Clerk's confessed veneration of Petrarch, this criticism seems out of character. Perhaps Chaucer, like the Host, is impatient to reach the story itself, without elaborate preliminaries.

55. *he wole conveyen his mateere* 'he wishes to introduce his story properly'.

56. *this his tale* 'this is his story'.
58. *the roote of Vesulus* 'the foot of Monte Viso'. The unusual expression represents Chaucer's literal translation of a phrase in Petrarch, 'ad radicem Vesuli'.
    the colde Monte Viso is over 12,000 feet high.
66. *ay redy to his hond* 'always attentive to his wishes'.
67. *bothe lasse and moore* 'both the common people and the nobility'.
68. *liveth, and hath doon yoore* 'lives, and has lived for a long time'. Brief changes of narrative tense to the present occur throughout this Tale (see, for example, lines 894, 897–8, 911).
71. *to speke as of linage* 'in point of ancestry'.
72. *gentilleste yborn* 'born of the noblest stock'.
73. *a fair persone* 'of good physique'.
74. *curteisie* A complex term whose senses include well-mannered behaviour, courtly elegance, nobility, generosity and goodness.
75. *his contree for to gye* 'to govern his kingdom'.
76. *he was to blame* 'he was at fault'.
79. *what mighte him bitide* 'what might happen to him' (viz., that he would grow old and die).
80. *on his lust present was al his thoght* 'his mind was completely taken up with pleasures of the moment'.
81. *as for to hauke* 'such as hawking'.
82. *wel ny alle othere cures leet he slide* 'he neglected almost all other demands upon his time'.
83. *eek he nolde* 'furthermore he would not'.
84. *for noght that may bifalle* 'whatever might happen'. The sentence includes three negatives—*nolde, no, noght*. Their effect is cumulative, conveying complete refusal.
85. *oonly that point* 'this failing alone'.
90. *koude he shewe wel swich mateere* 'he knew how best to present such a petition'. The sense of the whole sentence is that the speaker was chosen either because he was wisest, or because the marquis was known to be willing to listen to him, or because he had a gift for expressing such things.
92–3. *youre humanitee asseureth us and yeveth us hardinesse* Compare 'Ton humanité, sire marquis, nous donne hardiesse' (*LG*).
94. *as ofte as time is of necessitee* 'whenever it becomes necessary'.

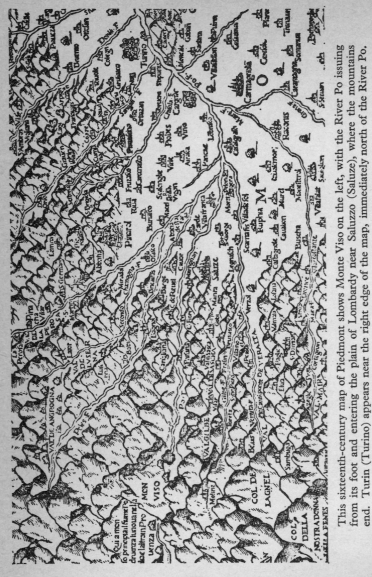

This sixteenth-century map of Piedmont shows Monte Viso on the left, with the River Po issuing from its foot and entering the plain of Lombardy near Saluzzo (Saluze), where the mountains end. Turin (Turino) appears near the right edge of the map, immediately north of the River Po.

95. *mowe telle oure hevinesse* 'may explain what is depressing us'.
96. *of youre gentillesse* 'out of your noble goodness'.
97. *with pitous herte* 'with troubled feelings'.
99–100. *al have I noght to doone . . . moore than another man* 'although this matter concerns me no more particularly than anyone else'.
101. *for as muche as* 'because'.
103–4. *a space of audience* 'a short hearing'.
105. *right as yow leste* 'exactly as it pleases you' (i.e. to accept our petition or not).
106–7. *us liketh yow and al youre werk* 'yourself and all that you do content us'.
108. *ne koude nat us self devisen* 'we could not imagine to ourselves'.
110. *if it youre wille be* 'if you would grant this'.
114. *of soverainetee, noght of servise* 'of authority, not of subordination'. The speaker assumes that the marquis will rule his wife, as indeed he does. This is the kind of masculine domination to which the Wife of Bath takes such exception. See lines 1170–2 below.
119. *it nil no man abide* 'it waits for no man'.
120. *as yit* 'at present'.
122. *deeth manaceth every age* 'death threatens men at every period of life'. Cp. 'Est la mort prochaine a tout aage, ne aucun ne lui eschappe' (*LG*).
122–3. *smyt in ech estaat* 'strikes every class of society'.
124. *al so certein* 'just as surely'.
130. *in short time atte leeste* 'as quickly as possible'.
131. *the gentilleste and the meeste* 'the noblest and most distinguished family'.
133. *as we kan deeme* 'as we judge'.
134. *bisy drede* 'anxiety'.
137. *youre linage sholde slake* 'your family should die out'. In the Middle Ages failure to beget an heir, and to provide for the succession, meant that a lord's subjects might find themselves fought over by rival claimants.
139. *wo were us alive !* 'how miserable our fate would be!'
143–4. *ye wol . . . to that I nevere erst thoughte streyne me* 'you are urging me to do something which I never contemplated'. Cp. 'Vous me contraignez, mes amis, a ce que je n'euz oncques en pensee' (*LG*).
145. *I me rejoised of* 'I took pleasure in'.

Notes

146. *that seelde time* 'which rarely'.
147. *ther I was free, I moot been in servage* 'where hitherto I had complete liberty, now I must be tied down'.
149. *wit* 'good judgement', 'intelligence'.
and have doon ay 'and always have done'.
151. *to wedde me* 'to get married'.
153–4. *I yow relesse that chois* 'I free you from the responsibility of choosing'. This is one of the few points of the tale at which Chaucer allows a note of irony to tinge the narrative.
156. *hir worthy eldres hem bifore* 'their noble ancestors'.
157. *bountee comth al of God* 'goodness comes entirely from God'. Chaucer uses the same argument in *The Wife of Bath's Tale*, 1109 ff. (see the notes to the edition in this series, p. 113). The argument appears in Petrarch, 'Quidquid in homine boni est, non ab alio quam a Deo est', but is not repeated in the *Livre Griseldis*.
160–1. *myn estaat and reste I him bitake* 'I commit my personal well-being and peace of mind to him'.
161. *as him leste* 'as it please him'.
164. *charge upon youre lyf* 'command most gravely'.
165. *what wyf that I take* 'whomever I marry'.
166. *whil that hir lyf may dure* 'as long as she lives'.
168. *as she* 'as though she'.
172. *as evere moot I thrive* 'as I hope to prosper'.
173. *ther as myn herte is set* 'I shall marry at the bidding of my heart' (i.e. for love, and not for a dowry or alliance with another noble family).
174. *but ye wole assente* 'unless you agree'.
176. *with hertely wil* 'with complete sincerity of purpose'. *Hertely* is not an adverb but the ME form of modern 'hearty'.
177. *to al this thing* 'to all these conditions'.
179–80. *a certein day of his spousaille* 'a definite date for his marriage'.
196. *to doon unto the feeste reverence* 'to dignify the celebrations'.
198. *shoop his mariage* 'planned to be married'.
199. *of site delitable* 'pleasantly situated'.
201. *hadden hir beestes and hir herbergage* 'lived and kept their livestock'.
202. *of hire labour tooke hir sustenance* 'won their living by working in the fields'.
203. *after that* 'according as'.

68

207. *a litel oxes stalle* Referring to the Nativity. Cp. 'Mais comme aucune foiz la grace de Dieu descent en un petit hostel et mainnaige' (*LG*).

212. *oon the faireste* 'one of the most beautiful'.

214. *no likerous lust was thurgh hire herte yronne* 'no unchaste thought crossed her mind'. Medieval physiology assumed that sexual impulses originated in the liver, the seat of blood. The sentence suggests that soft living breeds wanton inclinations.

215. *wel ofter of the welle than of the tonne* 'much more frequently water than wine'. A similar remark is made of the poor widow in *The Nun's Priest's Tale*.

216. *for she wolde vertu plese* 'because she wished to live virtuously'.

218. *tendre of age* 'still young'.

219–20. *yet in the brest of hire virginitee ther was enclosed ripe and sad corage* Cp. 'Toutesfoiz courage meur et ancien estoit muciez et enclos en sa virginité' (*LG*). Griselda's *ripe and sad corage* is a mature and constant spirit; but *ripe* in association with *brest* and *virginitee* also suggests her readiness for marriage.

221. *reverence and charitee* 'respect and love'.

223. *spinninge* While shepherding her flock, Griselda occupied herself usefully.

    on feeld 'at pasture'.

224. *til she slepte* 'until night'.

226. *wortes or othere herbes* Cp. 'Et au retour apportoit des chouz ou autre maniere d'erbettes pour eulx vivre' (*LG*).

227. *shredde and seeth for hir livinge* 'slice and boil for their food'.

228. *nothing softe* 'not at all comfortable'.

231. *to fadres reverence* 'out of respect for her father'.

234. *on hunting* 'while hunting'.

235. *whan it fil that he mighte hire espie* 'whenever he chanced to see her'.

236. *with wantown looking of folie* 'with lustful gaze'. This sense of *folie* persisted until the seventeenth century (see *Othello* v. 2. 133, 'She turned to folly, and she was a whore').

237. *in sad wise* 'gravely'.

238. *he wolde him ofte avise* 'he would often reflect'.

241. *of so yong age* 'so youthful'.

    as wel in chiere as dede 'as much in looks as in behaviour'.

242–3. *the peple have no greet insight in vertu* 'the common people have no proper understanding of moral goodness'.

243–4. *he considered ful right hir bountee* 'he judged her truly virtuous'.

247. *what womman that it sholde be* 'which woman he had chosen'.

250. *leve his vanitee* 'give up his irresponsible levity'.

253. *hath doon make* 'has had made'.

255. *for Grisildis sake* 'on Griselda's account', 'for her use'.

257. *lyk to hire stature* 'of similar build'.

259. *sholde falle* 'should appertain, as befitting the occasion'.

260. *the time of undren* 'nine o'clock in the morning'. This term could also mean mid-morning, noon, and mid-afternoon, but Petrarch's 'Hora iam prandii aderat' shows what is meant here.

263. *ech in his degree* 'every room decorated according to its importance'.

264. *houses of office* 'storerooms', 'cellars'.

265. *of deyntevous vitaille* 'with choice food'.

266. *as fer as last Itaille* 'as far as Italy extends'.

269. *the whiche that* 'those whom'.

270. *bachelrie* 'Bachelors' were landless knights who followed and fought for a great lord, in the hope of eventually being given a grant of land. These are the *privee knightes and squieres* of line 192.

273. *the righte wey han holde* 'went in procession along the road'.

275. *for hire shapen was al this array* 'these preparations were all intended for her'.

276. *is went* 'is gone'.

282. *that been my felawes* 'who are my friends'.

283–4. *fonde to doon* 'try to finish'.

285. *the labour which that longeth unto me* 'my appointed work'.

289. *gan hire for to calle* 'called her'. The auxiliary *gan* has the same function as 'did' in modern English. See also line 292 below.

291. *biside the thresshfold, in an oxes stalle* The close proximity of human beings and livestock in a medieval village explains why Chaucer links together *hir beestes and hir herbergage* in line 201 above. The mention of an ox's stall recalls the religious allusion in line 207 above. The *Livre Griseldis* mentions 'une croche de l'eaue', but does not specify the place.

294. *til she had herd what was the lordes wille* In her quiet submission to this noble visitor, so unexpected in her humble surroundings, Griselda recalls the Virgin of the Annunciation. 'And Mary said, "Behold, the handmaid of the Lord."'

298. *in humble cheere* 'humbly'.

299. *al redy* 'at your disposal'.

303. *whan he him hadde aside* 'having taken him aside'.

306. *if that thou vouche sauf* 'if you permit'.

308. *as for my wyf* 'to be my wife'.

310. *art my feithful lige man* Refers to the duty of the feudal tenant to his lord.

311. *al that liketh me* 'everything that suits me'.

313. *tel me that point* 'answer the proposal'.

316. *this sodeyn cas* 'this unexpected development'.

318. *unnethes seyde he wordes mo* 'he could hardly say another word'.

319–20. *my willinge is as ye wole* 'my wishes follow your desire'.

322. *right as yow lust, governeth this mateere* 'determine this matter exactly as it pleases you'.

323. *yet wol I* 'yet I wish'.

326. *for I wol axe* 'because I wish to ask'.

327. *reule hire after me* 'follow my bidding'.

329. Though Janicula submits to the marquis as to his lord, the marquis wishes also to show respect to Janicula, as to the father of his intended wife.

330–1. *aboute hir tretis* 'engaged upon her marriage-contract'.

332. *unto the hous withoute* 'They stood about, outside the house'.

333. *and wondred hem in how honest manere* 'and were astonished at how decently'.

335. *outrely Grisildis wondre mighte* 'most of all could Griselda feel astonished'.

336. *nevere erst* 'never before'.

341. *this matere for to chace* 'to wind up the subject'. Cp. line 393 below.

345. *it liketh to* 'it pleases'. The marquis courteously mentions the father first.

346. *it may so stonde* 'it may be the case'.

347. *ye wol that it so be* 'you wish this to happen'.

349. *in hastif wise* 'hastily', 'without due preparation'.

350. *or elles yow avise* 'or think it over'; with the implication of declining the offer.

351–2. *with good herte to al my lust* 'cheerfully to carry out all my wishes'.

352. *and that I frely may* 'and the things which I may do of right'.

353. *as me best thinketh* 'as seems best to me'.

   do yow laughe or smerte 'whether it give you pleasure or pain'.

354. *nevere ye to grucche it* 'without ever complaining'.

358. *this word* 'these words', 'this proposal'.

361. *as ye wole youreself* 'as you yourself desire this'.

364. *for to be deed* 'if it cost me my life'.

366. *with a ful sobre cheere* 'with a settled expression'.

372. *for that no thing of hir olde geere* 'so that none of her old garments'. The *Livre Griseldis* does not explain why she was stripped, but Petrarch has 'Hinc ne quid reliquiarum fortune veteris novam inferret in domum'. This complete change of clothing is a feature of the folk-tale upon which the Griselda story is based. It may originally have represented a change from mortal to fairy dress, which would explain why Griselda must surrender every part of it when she returns to everyday life.

374. *dispoillen hire right theere* 'strip off her clothes there and then'.

375. *nat right glad* 'not at all pleased'.

379. *hir heris han they kembd* 'they combed her hair'.

382. *sette hire ful of nowches* 'covered her with jewelled ornaments'.

383. *what sholde I?* 'why should I?'

385. *whan she translated was in swich richesse* 'when she was transformed into so rich a figure'. Cp. 'comme soudainement transmuee et changié, a paine la recongnust le peuple' (*LG*).

388. *wel ambling* 'moving easily and sedately'. Griselda would have little experience of riding.

389. *er he lenger lette* 'without more delay'.

396. *it ne semed nat by liklinesse* 'to no appearance did it seem'. Cp. 'Non pas en povre maison de villaige mais en hostel royal sembloit estre nourrie et avoir esté nee' (*LG*).

397. *born and fed in rudenesse* 'humbly born and brought up'.

401. *ther she was bore* 'from the village where she had been born'.

403. *unnethe trowed they* 'they could hardly believe'.

   dorste han swore 'dare have sworn' (that she was not Janicula's daughter).

405. *as by conjecture* 'judging by appearances'.

406. *hem thoughte* 'it seemed to them'.

409. *of thewes goode, yset in heigh bountee* 'her good manners set off by her virtuousness'.

410–13. Cp. 'Tant avoit en elle de honnesteté, belle vie, bonne maniere, sagesse, et douceur de parler que chascun se delittoit a la ouӱr' (*LG*).

411. *digne of reverence* 'worthy of respect'.

414. *of Saluces in the toun* 'in the city of Saluzzo'.

417. *if oon seyde wel* 'if one person spoke well of her'.

420. *upon hire to biholde* 'to gaze at her'.

422. *wedded with fortunat honestetee* 'gaining honour and happiness through his marriage'. Here Chaucer has preferred Petrarch's reading, 'ac prospero matrimonio honestatis', to that of the *Livre Griseldis*, 'humblement mais virtueusement mariez'.

424. *outward grace* 'with success in his public affairs'.

428. *wit* 'intelligence', 'wide knowledge'.

429. *koude al the feet of wyfly hoomlinesse* 'knew how to carry out all the duties of a housewife'.

431. *the commune profit koude she redresse* 'she knew how to put right grievances affecting the public well-being'. Cp. 'Ou le cas le requeroit, la chose publique adresçoit et pourveoit' (*LG*).

432. *ther nas discord* 'there was no disharmony'.

433. *that she ne koude apese* 'which she was not able to settle'.

436. *gentil men* 'nobles'.

437. *she wolde bringen hem aton* 'she would reconcile them'.

440. *that she from hevene sent was* Cp. 'Plusieurs la tenoient et disoient estre envoiee des cielz au salut du bien commun publique' (*LG*).

444. *al had hire levere have born a knave child* 'although she would have preferred a son'. Robinson remarks that *al had hire levere* is a confusion of *hire were levere* and *she had levere*.

446. *coome al bifore* 'arrive first'.

447. *she may unto a knave child atteyne* 'she may later produce a son'.

449. *ther fil* 'it happened'.
      times mo 'sometimes', 'now and then'.

6-2

450. *souked but a throwe* 'been suckled only a short while'. Petrarch has 'cum iam ablactata esset infantula', meaning that the event took place after the child had been weaned. This makes better sense of the story. Griselda's son is taken from her at the age of two (see lines 617–18 below).

452. *hir sadnesse for to knowe* 'to discover how constant she was'; referring to Griselda's undertakings before her marriage.

455. *nedelees, God woot* 'without reason, God knows'. As pointed out above in the Introduction, Chaucer is trying to provide a rational explanation for behaviour which, in folktales on this theme, was accountable by the other-worldly nature of the husband. His protests in the stanza following show a misunderstanding of the constancy test which he shares with Petrarch and Boccaccio.

459. *for a subtil wit* 'as an ingenious plan'. The appeal to the reader's sympathies in lines 457–62 has no counterpart in Chaucer's immediate sources.

460. *ivele it sit* 'it ill befits'.

463. *wroghte in this manere* 'did as follows'.

465. *with ful trouble cheere* 'looking deeply disturbed'.

468. *putte yow in estaat of heigh noblesse* 'raised you to a state of nobility'.

469. *as I gesse* 'I suppose'.

472. *maketh yow nat foryetful for to be* 'does not make you forget'.

473. *in povre estaat ful lowe* 'from the poorest social class'.

474. *for any wele ye moot youreselven knowe* 'whether for any profit, you yourself must know'. Griselda brought no dowry (see line 865 below).

480. *unto my gentils ye be no thing so* 'my nobles do not like you at all'.

482. *been in servage* 'to be subordinate to'.

488. *I may nat in this caas be recchelees* 'I cannot afford to act irresponsibly in this matter'.

490. *nat as I wolde* 'not as I wish myself'.

492–3. *withoute youre witing I wol nat doon* 'I do not wish to act without your knowledge'.

494. *ye to me assente as in this thing* 'give me your consent in this matter'.

495. *in youre werking* 'in your behaviour'.

496. *that ye me highte* 'that you promised to me'.

Notes

498. *she noght ameved* 'she did not change at all'.

501. *al lyth in youre plesaunce* 'your wishes must decide everything'.

502. *with hertely obeisaunce* 'with heart-felt submission'.

503–4. *ye mowe save or spille youre owene thing* 'you have the power of life and death over your own possessions'.

504. *werketh after youre wille* 'do as you privately wish'.

505–6. *ther may no thing . . . liken to yow that may displese me* 'nothing which pleased you could possibly give me offence'.

508. *ne drede for to leese* 'nor do I fear to lose anything'.

511. *ne chaunge my corage to another place* 'nor weaken my resolution'.

514. *al drery was his cheere* 'his face full of gloom': cp. 'courroucié et triste' (*LG*).

515. *whan that he sholde . . . go* 'as he left'.

516. *a furlong wey or two* 'within a little while': the third unnecessary phrase used to fill out this stanza. Like *as he were nat so* and *and his looking*, it merely repeats the sense of the preceding phrase.

519. *a maner sergeant* 'a kind of sergeant', or armed attendant. In the *Livre Griseldis* he is described as 'un sien serviteur et sergent a lui feable'.

520. *the which that* 'whom'.

521. *thinges grete* 'important affairs'.

522. *doon execucioun in thinges badde* 'carry out evil designs'.

523. *that he him loved* 'that the sergeant was his loyal servant'.

525. *he stalked him ful stille* 'he strode in without a word'.

527. *though I do thing* 'if I perform a deed'.

529. *lordes heestes mowe nat been yfeyned* 'a master's commands may not be shirked or evaded'.

530. *they mowe wel been biwailled or compleyned* 'they may indeed be regretted or lamented'.

531. *men moote nede unto hire lust obeye* 'servants must carry out their master's pleasure'.

533. *this child I am comanded for to take* By a curious chance, the speech of the sergeant in the *Livre Griseldis* also falls into a decasyllabic line: 'Commandé m'est de prandre cest enffant.'

534. *out the child he hente* 'plucked the child out of its cradle'.

535. *gan a cheere make* 'making such an expression'.

75

540. *suspecious was the diffame* 'doubtful was the reputation'. Chaucer is now following Petrarch very closely: 'Suspecta viri fama, suspecta facies, suspecta hora, suspecta erat oratio.' By so doing, he makes the Clerk ignore the Host's prohibition of rhetorical figures.

542. *the time in which he this bigan* Petrarch's phrase, 'suspecta hora', means that dead of night is not the time for honest deeds. Unlike Petrarch and his French translator, Chaucer does not say explicitly that the sergeant visited Griselda at night, though line 560 suggests this.

544. *right tho* 'at once'.

546. *conforminge hire to that the markis liked* 'adapting herself to whatever pleased the marquis'.

550. *that she moste kisse* 'that she might kiss'. Chaucer is exploiting the pathos of the situation by adding incidents to the story. In the *Livre Griseldis* the heroine's actions are reported in plain factual terms: 'Et de plain front prist son enffant et le regarda un pou et le baisa et beneist, et fist le signe de la croix, et le bailla audit sergent.' Chaucer expands this sentence to three stanzas, adding much that is graphic and making Griselda herself describe what she is doing, always with the main purpose of exciting pity. See especially lines 560 and 561–3, which have no counterpart in the sources.

560. *for my sake* 'on my account'; referring to the people's supposed dislike of her. Cp. 'for Grisildis sake', line 255.

561. *to a norice in this cas* 'to a nurse in such a situation' (who would feel distress at losing the child, but not a mother's grief).

564. *so sad stidefast* 'so unmoving in her constancy'.

567. *youre litel yonge maide* As Griselda complies with the marquis' wishes she ceases to speak of the child as her own.

570. *but my lord forbad* 'unless my husband commanded otherwise'.

572. *that beestes ne no briddes it torace* 'that no wild animals or birds may tear it to pieces'.

577. *point for point, in short and pleyn* 'in every particular, concisely and directly'.

579. *routhe in his manere* 'pity in his disposition'; meaning that he felt compassion.

580. *his purpos heeld he stille* 'he kept to his plan'.

584. *with alle circumstances* 'with everything the child needed'.

586. *upon peyne his heed of for to swappe* 'upon penalty of having his head struck off'.

590. *Panik* Panico, a noble family mentioned by Boccaccio and Petrarch, having estates near and within Bologna. Chaucer seems to have mistaken Panico for a place-name.

591. *shewe hire this mateere* 'explain his plan to her'.

592. *doon hire bisinesse* 'make it her special care'.

593. *to fostre in alle gentillesse* 'to bring up as a child of noble birth'.

595. *for oght that may bitide* 'no matter what should happen'.

598. *ful faste imagining* 'busily wondering'.

602. *evere in oon ylike* 'always the same'.
     sad and kinde 'constant and loving'.

603. *as glad, as humble, as bisy in servise* Here Chaucer takes over a rhetorical figure from the *Livre Griseldis*: 'telle lesce, telle obeissance, tel service et amour.'

605. *in every maner wise* 'in every possible way'.

607. *noon accident, for noon adversitee* 'no outward sign of any grief she suffered'.

608–9. *ne nevere . . . ne nempned she* 'nor did she ever mention'.

609. *in ernest nor in game* 'neither seriously nor in jest'; under no circumstances. Cp. *The General Prologue*, line 534: 'thogh him gamed or smerte'.

610. *ther passed been foure yeer* 'four years passed'.

611. *as God wolde* 'as it pleased God'.

612. *a knave child she bar by this Walter* 'she bore Walter a son'.

617–18. *fro the brest departed of his norice* 'weaned'. It was not usual for courtly ladies to suckle their children.

619. *caughte yet another lest* 'felt another desire'.

620. *to tempte his wyf yet ofter* 'to test his wife yet again'.
     if he may 'if he could'.

621. *tempted in assay* 'put to the test'.

622. *ne knowe no mesure* 'recognize no restraint'.

624. *er this* 'on a previous occasion'.

625. *sikly berth* 'grudgingly accept'.

626. *namely sith my sone yboren is* 'especially since the birth of my son'.

627. *evere in al oure age* 'at any time since our marriage'.

628. *sleeth myn herte and my corage* 'demoralizes me'. In this context *herte* and *corage* are indistinguishable in sense.

629. *so smerte* 'so painfully'.

632. *the blood of Janicle* 'Janicula's descendant'.

635. *wel oughte I* 'I must'.

637. *though they nat pleyn speke in myn audience* 'though they don't say this directly in my hearing'.

639. *disposed outrely* 'firmly decided'.

640. *servede by nighte* 'treated under cover of night'.

643. *out of youreself for no wo sholde outreye* 'should not become hysterical through grief'.

644. *and therof I yow preye* 'I beseech you'.

646. *I wol no thing, ne nil no thing* 'I do not wish, nor will I ever desire, anything'.

647. *but as yow list* 'except as pleases you'.

650. *I have noght had no part of children tweyne* 'I have had nothing of my two children'. Here, as Chaucer accents the pathos of her speech, Griselda comes close to complaining. Her counterpart in the *Livre Griseldis* is more matter-of-fact: 'Ne je n'ay riens en ces enffans que l'enffantement.'

651. *siknesse* 'the discomfort of pregnancy'.

652. *dooth with youre owene thing* 'dispose of your possessions': the same reply as Griselda gives in lines 503–4 above.

653. *axeth no reed at me* 'don't consult me'.

663. *al youre plesance ferme and stable I holde* 'I remain entirely constant to your wishes'.

664. *do yow ese* 'please you'.

667. *unto youre love* The French translation makes Griselda refer to 'nostre amour'. Chaucer's phrase makes her touchingly dependent upon her lord's affection.

677. *evere in oon* 'just the same', 'as before'.

678. *no chiere maade of hevinesse* 'gave no sign of grief'.

681. *in erthe grave* 'bury'.

685. *as him no thing ne roghte* 'as though it were a matter of no consequence to him'.

687. *evere lenger the moore* 'increasingly'.

691. *he wolde have wend that of som subtiltee* 'he would have supposed that out of cunning'.

692. *crueel corage* 'cruelty of heart'.

696. *wolde I axen fain* 'I should like to ask'. Chaucer is again close to the French translation: 'Povoient, je vous prie, a ce seigneur ces experimens d'obeïssance et de foy de mariage bien souffire?'

700. *continuinge evere in sturdinesse* 'persisting in cruelty'.

701. *folk of swich condicion* 'people of such nature'. Cp. 'Mais y sont aucuns que quant il ont aucune chose com-

mancié ou en propos qui continuent tousjours plus' (*LG*).
This sentence provides Chaucer with the matter of lines
701–3, after which he completes the stanza by developing
the point in his own way. This illustrates the remark made by
Sisam in his edition of *The Clerk's Tale*, p. xxi, that where
Chaucer's additions run to less than a stanza, the new matter
appears almost invariably at the stanza's end.

702. *a certein purpos take* 'determined on a particular course'.

704. *right as* 'just as if'.

708. *he waiteth* 'he waits to see': another sudden shift to
present tense.

709. *changed of corage* 'weakened in spirit'.

711. *ay oon* 'always the same'.

712–13. *ay the forther . . . the moore trewe* 'the older she grew,
the more faithful she became'. Cp. line 687 above, 'evere
lenger the moore'.

715. *of hem two* 'between the two of them'.

718. *al fil* 'everything turned out'.

719. *for no worldly unreste* 'that, whatever her trouble'.

720–1. *a wyf, as of hirself, nothing ne sholde wille in effect* 'a wife
should wish nothing to happen for her own gratification'.

721. *but as hir housbonde wolde* 'but in the way her husband
desires it'.

731. *made hem that they him hatede* 'caused the people to
hate him'.

733. *for ernest ne for game* 'for no cause, whatever the circumstances'. Cp. line 609 above.

734. *nolde stente* 'would not stop'.

737. *the court of Rome* The papal court to which all matters of
divorce were referred.

    in subtil wise 'cleverly'.

738. *message* 'messenger', 'ambassador'.

739. *swiche bulles to devise* 'to invent such mandates from the
Pope'. This detail of the story cannot pretend to be convinc-
ing. A supernatural husband could test his mortal wife's
constancy without any such mock appeal to ecclesiastical
authority, especially if—as in *Le Freine* and *Fair Annie*—he
had not yet married her.

740. *may suffise* 'would answer'.

743. *I seye* This second account of the circumstances suggests
that Chaucer's grasp of the narrative is not very sure at this
point.

744. *makinge mencion* 'declaring'.

746. *as by* 'by virtue of'.

749. *publiced atte fulle* 'made known in detail'.

751. *it hadde be right so* 'that it were indeed so'.

753. *ful wo* 'grief-stricken'.

754. *ylike sad for everemo* 'remaining constant as ever'.

759. *as to hire verray worldly suffisance* 'as though Walter were her entire worldly happiness'.

774. *at day set* 'on the appointed day'.

778. *toward hir mariage* 'in preparation for her marriage'.

779. *ful of gemmes cleere* 'beset with sparkling gems'.

784. *they riden in hir wey* 'they ride towards Saluzzo'.

787. *the outtreste preeve of hir corage* 'the supreme test of her spirit'.

792. *I hadde ynogh plesance* 'I was considerate enough'.

793. *to my wyf* 'as wife'.

794. *as for youre trouthe* 'for your fidelity'.

796. *in verray soothfastnesse* 'in truth indeed'; literally, 'in veritable truth'.

797. *if I wel avise* 'if I consider carefully'.

798. *greet servitute in sondry wise* 'great servitude in many respects'. Cp. 'Toute grande fortune et seigneurie est grant servitute' (*LG*).

800-1. *my peple me constreyneth for to take another wyf* 'my people urge me to marry again'. Cp. 'Mes gens me contraignent . . . que je preigne une autre femme' (*LG*).

802. *rancour for to slake* 'to put an end to this bad feeling'.

805. *by the weye* 'along the road'.

806. *voide anon hir place* 'vacate her place at once'. In the *Livre Griseldis* the marquis puts the request more gently: 'Fay lieu a l'autre.' Chaucer is continuing to make Walter harsh and unfeeling.

808. *I graunte it of my grace* 'I allow it you as a mark of favour'. As Griselda indicates in her reply, lines 848-50 below, Walter is being unpleasantly sardonic.

811. *with evene herte I rede yow t'endure* 'I advise you to suffer with unmoved feelings'.

813. *she again answerde* 'she replied'. Griselda's reply corresponds very closely with the parallel passage of the *Livre Griseldis*. The two passages are reproduced side by side as an Appendix on pp. 92-6 below.

816. *no wight kan ne may* 'nobody could or should'.

817. *it is no nay* 'this is beyond question'.

818. *I ne heeld me nevere digne* 'I never considered myself worthy'.

822. *also wysly he my soule glaade* 'as surely as I hope for salvation'; literally, 'as surely as may God comfort my soul'.

823. *I nevere heeld me* 'I never thought of myself as'.

825. *whil that my lyf may dure* 'as long as I live'.

826. *aboven every worldly creature* 'respecting him before every other person'.

829. *where as I was noght worthy* 'when I was unworthy'.

831. *foryelde it yow* 'reward you for it'.

834. *ther I was fostred of a child ful smal* 'where I was brought up as a child'.

836. *a widwe clene in body* 'a widow living chastely'.

839. *God shilde swich a lordes wyf to take* 'God forbid that the wife of so great a man should take'.

840. *or to make* 'or as mate'. The Wife of Bath would not relish this sentiment (see her Prologue, lines 46–50).

844. *in which that I was blisful wont to bee* 'in which I have been so happy'.

847. *that I shal goon, I wol goon whan yow leste* 'that I should go, I wish to go when it pleases you'.

848. *but ther as ye me profre* 'but when you offer me'.

850. *nothing faire* 'not at all attractive'.

851. *the whiche to me were hard now for to finde* 'which it would be difficult for me to find now'. But see lines 913–17 below.

852. *O goode God!* The outburst of poignant feeling in lines 852–4 adds pathos to the story at the price of upsetting Griselda's composure. It has no counterpart in the French version of the tale (see p. 94 below).

855. *sooth is seyd* 'it is truly said'.

856. *in effect* 'in its working'.

857. *love is noght oold as whan that it is newe* 'when it grows old, love is no longer what it was when new'.

858. *for noon adversitee* 'whatever misfortune befall me'.

859. *to dyen in the cas* 'though it were to kill me'.

861. *in hool entente* 'completely'.

862. *fadres place* 'father's house'.

867. *restoore* 'give back'.

870. *dar I saufly sayn* 'I am sure': like *of youre grace* and *out of drede* in the previous stanza, a phrase unnecessary to the sense, which serves to complete a rhyming line.

872. *naked moot I turne again* 'naked must I return'. The remark hints at religious significances behind the story (cp. Job i. 21, and line 923 below).

873. *wol I folwen fain* 'I wish very much to carry out'.

875. *that I smoklees out of youre paleys wente* 'that I should leave your palace without a single garment'.

876. *dishonest* 'dishonourable'.

877. *thilke wombe* 'this belly'.

880. *lyk a worm* 'naked'; a stock comparison. See the description of Poverty in Chaucer's *Romaunt of the Rose*, line 454: 'nakid as a worm was she'.

883. *in gerdon of my maidenhede* 'in return for my virginity'.

884. *noght again I bere* 'I do not carry back again'.

885. *as voucheth sauf to yeve me* 'consent to grant me': *as* being used to introduce an imperative.

887. *wrye the wombe of here* 'cover the belly of the woman'; by implication, her nakedness.

889. *lest I yow greve* 'in case I annoy you by remaining longer'.

891. *lat it be stille* 'leave it there'.

892. *wel unnethes* 'with great difficulty'.

893. *for routhe and for pitee* 'for compassion'. The phrase belongs with *unnethes . . . he spak* in the previous line.

894. *hirselven strepeth she* Griselda takes off her robe herself, without the help of attendant ladies. The form *hirselven* is the inflected accusative.

896. *hir fadre hous* Cp. *hir doghter name* in line 608 above. In both instances Chaucer is using the uninflected genitive form, which survived from OE until the fifteenth century.

897. *wepinge in hir weye* 'weeping as they followed her'.

900. *ne spak she noon* 'she spoke not a word'.

903. *shoop him to been a lives creature* 'made him a living creature': thus he cursed the day he was born. The same expression occurs in *Troilus and Criseyde*, iv. 251–2:

> Acorsed be that day which that Nature
> Shoop me to be a lives creature.

905. *in suspect* 'mistrustful'.

906. *sith that it bigan* 'from the beginning'.

907. *fulfild hadde his corage* 'satisfied his sexual desire'.

908. *him wolde thinke* 'it would seem to him'.

909. *so lowe for t'alighte* 'to settle upon so base a partner'.

910. *voiden hire* 'get rid of her'.

911. *agains* 'towards, in order to meet'.

913. *as it mighte be* 'as much as possible'.

914. *ful sorwefully wepinge* A pathetic touch not found in Petrarch or in the *Livre Griseldis*.

915. *mighte he it nat bringe* 'he could not draw the garment'.

916. *rude was the clooth, and moore of age* 'the garment was ill-fitting and much older'. Chaucer does not follow the more realistic explanation of the French translator that Griselda 'estoit devenue grande et embarnie'.

918. *for a certeyn space* 'for a period of time'.

921. *ne eek in hire absence* 'nor by avoiding company'.

922. *that hire was doon offence* 'that she had been wrongfully treated'.

924. *as by hire contenaunce* 'to judge by her complexion'.

925. *in hire grete estaat* 'during her life as a noblewoman'.

926. *hire goost was evere in pleyn humilitee* 'she had always shown great humility of spirit'.

927. *no tendre mouth* 'with no taste for fine food'.
     noon herte delicaat 'not caring for luxury'.

928. *no semblant of roialtee* 'no show of magnificence'.

930. *discreet and pridelees* 'self-effacing and modest'.

932. *moost for his humblesse* 'especially of his humility'.

934. *namely of men* 'especially about men'.
     as in soothfastnesse 'to speak truth'.

935. *clerkes preise wommen but a lite* The Wife of Bath makes the same observation, but by way of complaint:

> For trusteth wel, it is an impossible
> That any clerk wol speke gode of wives,
> But if it be of hooly seintes lives,
> Ne of noon oother womman never the mo. (687–90)

For the Clerk to admit the justice of the complaint seems to confirm that Chaucer did not have him in mind as narrator when he wrote the Tale.

938. *but it be falle of newe* 'unless it has happened very recently' (unknown to the speaker). Again the remark hardly suits the Clerk.

940. *the fame up sprang to moore and lesse* 'the news spread round to rich and poor'.

941. *alle and some* 'one and all', 'everyone'.

942. *was kouth eek* 'was it also known'.

946. *which that shoop* 'who had planned'.

950. *nat with no swollen thoght in hire corage* 'without any haughtiness of spirit'.

951. *on hire knees hire sette* 'kneeled down'.

952. *wisely she him grette* 'she greeted him respectfully'.

953. *my wil is outrely* 'it is my firm intention'.

957–8. *every wight in his degree have his estaat* 'every guest be received and treated in accordance with his rank'. Cp. 'Que chascun soit festoyé et ordonné selon sa personne et estat' (*LG*).

958. *in sitting and servise* 'in respect of his place and attendance'.

959. *as I kan best devise* 'to my best ability'.

960–1. *suffisaunt . . . the chambres for t'arraye in ordinaunce* 'capable of putting the rooms in fit order'.

962. *after my lust* 'according to my wish'.

963. *that thyn were al swich manere governaunce* 'that you should take charge of all such matters'.

965. *ivel biseye* 'ill-provided': cp. 'mal vestue et povrement' (*LG*).

966. *at the leeste weye* 'at the very least'.

968. *to doon youre lust* 'to carry out your wishes'.

969. *in my degree* 'in my lowly fashion'.

971. *for no wele ne no wo* 'for no cause of any kind'.

972. *the goost withinne myn herte* 'the spirit in my breast'.

974–8. *and with that word . . . swepe and shake* Cp. 'Et en ce disant, commence a besoingnier, comme de baloier la maison, mettre tables, faire liz, et ordonner tout et prier aux autres chamberieres que chascune en droit soy feist au mieulx qu'elle pourroit' (*LG*).

976. *peyned hire to doon al that she mighte* 'strained herself to do her utmost'.

980. *his halle* 'the great hall of the palace'.

981. *abouten undren* 'about nine in the morning'.

985. *and thanne at erst* 'and then for the first time'.

990. *fairer fruit bitwene hem sholde falle* 'more attractive children would spring from them'.

991. *for hire heigh linage* 'on account of her high birth'.

993. *hem to seen the peple hath caught plesaunce* 'joy seized the people at the sight of them'.

994. *governaunce* 'management of affairs'.

995–1008. *O stormy peple !* These two stanzas appear to be a later interpolation. The more vigorous style of the passage, with its proverbial expressions and colloquial energy, suggests the final phase of Chaucer's poetic development. Such phrases as *chaunginge as a fane*, *rumbul that is newe*, *lyk the moone*, *deere ynogh a jane*, and *a ful greet fool*, stand apart from the general style of *The Clerk's Tale*, though much akin to the vernacular roughness of *The Clerk's Prologue*. Some political event of the troubled closing years of Richard II's reign may have prompted this outburst of contempt for the fickleness of the common people. Its anger is uncharacteristic of Chaucer.

995. *unsad and evere untrewe* 'forever inconstant and fickle'.

996. *chaunginge as a fane* 'changeable as a weathervane'.

997. *rumbul that is newe* 'fresh rumour'.

999. *ay ful of clapping* 'always gossiping and chattering'. Cp. line 1200 below: 'Ay clappeth as a mille.'

deere ynogh a jane 'not worth a ha'penny'.

1000. *youre doom is fals* 'your judgement is misguided'.

1001. *that on yow leeveth* 'who trusts in you'.

1002. *sadde folk* 'discerning people'.

1004. *right for the noveltee* 'simply for the novelty'.

1005. *a newe lady of hir toun* 'a new marchioness in Saluzzo'.

1007. *wol I me dresse* 'will I turn'. Chaucer admits interrupting his story.

1011. *right noght was she abaist of hire clothing* 'she was not at all embarrassed by her wretched clothes'. Cp. 'sans avoir honte de ce qu'elle estoit si mal vestue' (*LG*). Chaucer's *abaist* seems to have been picked up from 'abaissié', which occurs in the same sentence.

1012. *rude and somdeel eek torent* 'shapeless and tattered'.

1014. *to greete the markisesse* Chaucer omits Griselda's courteous words of welcome to her supposed successor, which both Petrarch and the French translator give.

1015. *dooth forth hire bisinesse* 'attends to her duties'.

1017. *everich in his degree* 'each one with appropriate ceremony'.

1019. *what she mighte bee* 'who she should be'.

1020–1. *that in so povre array . . . koude swich honour* 'who, despite her wretched dress, had such expert knowledge of courtly etiquette'. Cp. 'Chascun . . . se merveilloient dont telles meurs, tant grant sens soubz tel abit venoient' (*LG*).

1022. *worthily they preisen hire prudence* 'they commended her admirable judgement'.

1023–4. *she ne stente . . . to commende* 'she did not cease to praise'.

1026. *no man koude hir pris amende* 'no one was able to surpass her commendation'.

1028. *to sitten doun to mete* 'to begin the feast'.

1030. *as it were in his pley* 'as though jocularly'.

1031. *how liketh thee my wyf?* 'what do you think of my wife?'

1033. *saugh I nevere noon* 'I never saw anyone'.

1038–41. *that ye ne prikke . . . moore tendrely* Cp. 'que tu ne la poingnes des aguillons que tu as pointe l'autre, car et plus jeune est et plus delicieusement nourrie' (*LG*).

1039. *as ye han doon mo* 'as you have done to others'; alluding indirectly to herself, and following the example of her French counterpart, who refers delicately to 'l'autre'.

1040. *fostred in hire norissinge* 'brought up'; a pleonasm.

1041. *to my supposinge* 'as I believe'.

1043. *a povre fostred creature* 'a person brought up in poverty' (like herself).

1048. *continuinge evere hire innocence overal* 'maintaining her moral goodness in every trial'.

1049–50. *this sturdy markis gan his herte dresse to rewen* 'this cruel marquis felt stirrings of pity'. These two lines, which Chaucer added to the story, show him again stressing the unkindness of Walter in order to make Griselda a more pathetic figure.

1052. *namoore agast ne ivele apayed* 'no longer alarmed or aggrieved'.

1054. *as wel as evere womman was, assayed* 'tested as rigorously as ever a woman was'.

1055. *in greet estaat, and povreliche arrayed* 'both as a noblewoman and as a poor person'.

1057. *gan hire kesse* 'kissed her'.

1058. *for wonder took of it no keep* 'in her amazement did not take it in'.

1060. *she ferde as* 'she behaved as though'.

1062. *that for us deyde* 'who died for us'.

1066. *that oother* 'the other child'.
feithfully 'truly'.

1068. *thou bare him in thy body trewely* 'he is indeed the child you bore'; or *trewely* may mean 'honourably'.

1071. *thou hast lorn noon* 'you have lost neither'.

1078. *til I thy purpos knewe* 'until I had made certain of your disposition'.

1079. *aswowne doun she falleth* 'she collapsed in a faint'.

1080. *for pitous joye* Chaucer's gloss on the bare phrase 'se laissa cheoir' in the *Livre Griseldis*. In Petrarch's version of the tale Griselda does not faint.

1081. *she bothe hire yonge children to hire calleth* The remainder of the stanza, and the four stanzas immediately following, represent Chaucer's own contribution to the tale. Petrarch describes Griselda's reunion with her children in a few words, telling how she 'wearied them with kisses and be-dewed them with her loving tears' (French, p. 310). The *Livre Griseldis* does not mention this physical reunion. Chaucer's vocabulary shows him intent upon wringing pathos out of the situation: see his repeated use of *pitous* (lines 1080, 1082, 1086, 1104), *tendrely* (lines 1083, 1093, 1097), *teeres* (lines 1084, 1104), and *wepinge* (line 1082), which set the emotional tone of the passage.

1086. *O which a pitous thing* 'what a touching sight'.

1088. *God thanke it yow* 'God give you thanks for it'.

1090. *rekke I nevere to been deed right heere* 'I should not care if I died this moment'.

1092. *no fors of deeth* 'death is of no importance'.

1094. *wende stedfastly* 'believed firmly'.

1098. *hath doon yow kept* 'have preserved you'.

1099. *she swapte adoun to grounde* 'she fell to the floor'. This second swoon weakens Chaucer's climax by insisting too much upon its pathos. Where Chaucer parts company with his source-story, he loses the restraint which it places upon his sentimental impulse.

1102. *with greet sleighte* 'by using stratagems'.

1103. *they gonne arace* 'they freed'.

1106. *mighte they abide* 'could they remain there'.

1107. *hire sorwe slaketh* 'soothes away her grief'.

1109. *hire joye and feeste maketh* 'shows her joy and respect'. This sentence is caught up from a later point of the French narrative, 'chascun commença a faire bonne chiere et joyeuse'. The rest of the stanza is original to Chaucer.

1110. *caught again hire contenaunce* 'recovered her composure'.

1111. *so feithfully plesaunce* 'show her such loving regard'.

1112–13. *the cheere bitwixe hem two* 'the happiness between them'.

1114. *whan that they hir time say* 'when they saw a suitable opportunity'. By interpolating so much after Griselda's original swoon, Chaucer misses the effective point made in the *Livre Griseldis*, where Griselda is stripped of her ragged clothes and put into noble dress while she is still unconscious.

1115. *into chambre* 'into a private room'.

1120. *as hire oghte* 'according to her due'.

1124. *on the welkne* 'in the vault of heaven'.

1125. *moore solempne* 'more stately and impressive'.

1126. *gretter of costage* 'more lavish and costly'.

1129. *in concord and in reste* 'in love and peace'.

1136. *after his fader day* 'after his father died'.

1138. *al putte he nat his wyf in greet assay* 'although he did not expose his wife to a painful trial'.

1140. *in olde times yoore* Referring to the legendary Golden Age. See Chaucer's unfinished poem, *The Former Age* (Robinson, p. 534).

1141. *this auctour* Petrarch, whose summing-up begins, 'Hanc historiam stilo nunc alio retexere visum fuit.' The French translator follows closely, as does Chaucer in lines 1142 ff. It was the misreading or mistranscription of the phrase 'stilo alio'—another language—as 'stilo alto', which was responsible for Chaucer's reference to 'heigh style', repeated in line 1148 below. Before printing, such slips were easily made.

1142. *nat for that* 'not in order that'.

1143. *folwen Grisilde as in humilitee* 'imitate Griselda's humility'.

1144. *it were inportable, though they wolde* 'it would prove impossible to bear, even if they wished to do so'.

1145. *in his degree* 'whatever his station'.

1150. *wel moore us oghte* 'so much the more should we'.

1152. *greet skile is* 'it is very reasonable'.
he preeve that he wroghte 'he should test what he created'.

1153. *he ne tempteth no man that he boghte* 'he tempts none of us whom he redeemed'.

1154. *as seith Seint Jame* See James i. 13: 'Let no man say when he is tempted, I am tempted of God; for God cannot be tempted with evil, neither tempteth he any man.'

1155. *he preeveth folk al day* 'he tests people all the time'.

1156. *as for oure excercise* 'for our spiritual trial'.

1159. *nat for to knowe oure wil* 'not in order to discover our strength of purpose'.

1161. *for oure beste is al his governaunce* 'his control of our lives is for our advantage'.

1162. *in vertuous suffraunce* 'with uncomplaining patience'.

1163. *but o word, lordinges* The remainder of the tale bears no relationship to Petrarch's story or to the *Livre Griseldis*, and was probably added when Chaucer came to draft his story into the body of *The Canterbury Tales*. As in lines 995–1001 above, there is a perceptible shift of style from courtly to colloquial and an assumption of an ironic tone, which characterize Chaucer's writing in such late works as the *General Prologue* and *The Wife of Bath's Prologue*. With *The Clerk's Prologue*, these closing fifty lines serve to bind the Tale into the broad setting of the wayside competition.

1165. *in al a toun* 'in a whole city'.

1167. *hath now so badde alayes* 'is now put into such inferior alloys'.

1168. *fair at ye* 'attractive in appearance'. *Ye* is disyllabic.

1169. *breste a-two than plie* 'snap in half than bend'.

1170. *for the Wives love of Bathe* 'out of respect for the Wife of Bath', whose Prologue advances a completely opposite view of sovereignty within marriage. In modern English a phrase is given its genitive form by inflecting the final noun, e.g. the Wife of Bath's Tale. ME inflected the name of the possessor, e.g. the Wives Tale of Bathe.

1171. *al hire secte* Either 'her whole sex' or 'all those women who uphold male subordination'; probably the latter.

1172. *in heigh maistrie* 'in overlordship'.

1174. *seyn yow* 'recite to you', or 'sing'.

1175. *lat us stinte of ernestful matere* 'let us put an end to this serious talk'. The remark does not suggest the sober gravity imputed to the Clerk in the *General Prologue*, but the writing of Chaucer's final period contains other such appeals against 'ernestful matere'. Cp. *The Nun's Priest's Tale*, line 391, 'Now let us speke of mirthe, and stinte al this', and the Host's remark in the Prologue to the same tale, 'It is a peyne . . . to heere of hevinesse'. It looks as though Chaucer, in this last phase of writing, was inclined towards the Host's taste for 'some murie thing', perhaps because comedy allowed him to give richer expression to his exuberant creative energy.

1177. *Grisilde is deed* At this point Chaucer substitutes for rhyme-royal a six-line stanza which employs only three rhymes, *-ience*, *-aille*, and *-inde*, throughout the series.

Chaucer sets himself a difficult technical feat, and brings it off triumphantly.

1180. *so hardy* 'so foolhardy'.

1181. *in trust to finde* 'in hope of finding'.

1184. *youre tonge naille* 'restrain your tongue'.

1185. *have cause or diligence* 'have cause or spend endeavour'. The rhyme is secured at some cost to the syntax.

1188. *Chichevache* A legendary cow which fed only on patient wives.

1189. *folweth Ekko* 'follow the example of Echo'.

1191. *bidaffed for youre innocence* 'fooled through your simplicity'.

1192. *taak on yow the governaille* 'assume the mastery'.

1194. *for commune profit sith it may availle* 'since it may contribute to the general good'.

1195. *stondeth at defense* 'take up arms to protect yourselves'.

1197. *ne suffreth nat that men yow doon offense* 'don't allow men to subject you to any indignity'.

1198. *sklendre wives, fieble as in bataille* 'wives who are physically small, and unable to offer bodily resistance'. The Wife of Bath achieves mastery over her fifth husband after knocking him over backwards into the fire.

1199. *beth egre as is a tigre* 'be fierce as a tiger'.

1200. *ay clappeth* 'nag ceaselessly'.

1201. *doth hem no reverence* 'pay them no respect'.

1204. *eek his aventaille* 'even his helmet'. The word seems to have been dictated by the rhyme, but is neatly justified by *armed be in maille* two lines earlier.

1205. *I rede eek thou him binde* 'I advise you to entrap him'.

1206. *couche as doth a quaille* 'crouch down, taking cover like a frightened quail'.

1207. *ther folk been in presence* 'where people gather in companies'.

1208. *and thyn apparaille* 'and your clothing'. The Wife of Bath needs no such advice: see her Prologue, lines 552–9.

1209. *if thou be foul, be fre of thy dispence* 'if you should be ugly, spend money lavishly'.

1210. *to gete thee freendes ay do thy travaille* 'do everything to make yourself popular'.

1211. *of chiere as light* 'as gay in manner'.

1212. *lat him care* 'let him worry'.

APPENDIX: CHAUCER'S USE OF
'LE LIVRE GRISELDIS'

Like several passages of *The Clerk's Tale*, lines 813–924 are closely modelled on the corresponding part of the *Livre Griseldis*. By setting the two texts side by side, we can watch Chaucer translating and reshaping French prose into English rhymed verse, varying the importance of incidents and altering the tone of the narrative. Comparison of the two versions shows that Chaucer follows the same order of events, and that each of his stanzas—except one with no counterpart in the French story—begins by adapting a sentence of this source. It also shows that sometimes Chaucer follows the *Livre Griseldis* for only three or four lines of his stanza, and that the remaining lines consist of new material added in order to round off the stanza as a unit of sense, and to complete the rhyme-scheme. The four lines 837–40 provide an example. The three opening lines of the stanza reproduce the substance of part of a long sentence in the *Livre Griseldis*, after which, instead of attempting to compress the next sentence into four lines of verse, Chaucer fills up the stanza with matter of his own. The passage 862–8, again, begins by closely following the French text, but after Chaucer has introduced the otiose phrase *out of drede* for the sake of rhyme, he is obliged to render 'foy et loyauté' as *feith, and nakednesse, and maidenhede*. In lines 869–75 he again begins by translating the French version, but then omits the passage 'et autres ornemens...me toust et reprent', apparently in order to make Griselda's striking remark, 'Nue vins de chiez mon pere, et nue la retourneray', stand in the middle of the stanza, where the rhymes are more easily arranged. He then leaves himself to complete the stanza with three lines of original material. Two stanzas later he completes his rendering of the sentence beginning 'Pour laquelle chose' in five and a half lines of verse, and rounds off the stanza by giving Griselda an extra remark, not found in the source. A little later he encounters a still shorter sentence of the *Livre Griseldis* which yields only the four lines 897–900; and then, to avoid accepting the toneless comment 'Et ainsy s'en retourna en l'ostel de son pere', Chaucer completes the stanza by inventing a new incident derived from his own *Troilus and Criseyde*.

Italicized lines and phrases denote Chaucer's additions to the French version of the story. The text of the *Livre Griseldis* is taken from J. B. Severs, *op. cit.* pp. 255–89.

And she again answerde in pacience,
'My lord,' quod she, 'I woot, and wiste alway,
815 How that bitwixen your magnificence
And my poverte no wight kan ne may
Maken comparison; *it is no nay.*
I ne heeld me nevere digne in no manere
To be youre wyf, no, ne youre chamberere.

820 'And in this hous, ther ye me lady maade—
The heighe God take I for my witnesse,
And also wysly he my soule glaade—
I nevere heeld me lady ne mistresse,
But humble servant to your worthinesse,
825 And evere shal, *whil that my lyf may dure,*
Aboven every worldly creature.

'That ye so longe of your benignitee
Han holden me in honour and nobleye,
Where as I was noght worthy for to bee,
830 That thonke I God and yow, *to whom I preye*
Foryelde it yow; ther is namoore to seye.
Unto my fader gladly wol I wende,
And with him dwelle unto my lives ende.

'Ther I was fostred of a child ful smal,
835 Til I be deed my lyf ther wol I lede,
A widwe clene in body, herte and al.
For sith I yaf to yow my maidenhede,
And am youre trewe wyf, it is no drede,
God shilde swich a lordes wyf to take
840 *Another man to housbonde or to make!*

A ce dist elle: 'J'ai tousjours sceu et tenu que entre ta grant magnificence et mon humilité et povreté n'avoit nulle comparoison, ne moy oncques[1] je ne dis mie seulement d'estre ta femme, mais d'estre ta chamberiere ne me reputay digne.

Et j'en appelle Dieu en tesmoing, qui scet[2] tout, en ceste tienne maison ou tu m'as fait dame, ay tousjours en cuer[3] et me suy tenue pour ta chamberiere et servente.

De ce temps, doncques, que sans mes merites et trop plus que je ne vail certainement moy honnourant j'ay esté avec toy, j'en rens graces a Dieu et a toy. Quant au remenant, je suy preste[4] de bon et prompt courage de retourner chiez mon pere,

ou j'ay esté nourrie en m'enfance; et d'y estre en ma villesce,[5] et la morir bien me plaist, bieneureuse et honnourable vesve[6] de si grant seigneur comme tu es.

---

[1] *oncques* = jamais. [2] *scet* = sait. [3] *cuer* = cœur.
[4] *preste* = prête. [5] *villesce* = vieillesse. [6] *vesve* = veuve.

'And of youre newe wyf God of his grace
So graunte yow wele and prosperitee!
For I wol gladly yelden hire my place,
In which that I was blisful wont to bee.

845 For sith it liketh yow, my lord,' quod shee,
'*That whilom weren al myn hertes reste,*
That I shal goon, I wol goon whan yow leste.

'But ther as ye me profre swich dowaire
As I first broghte, it is wel in my minde

850 *It were my wrecched clothes, nothing faire,*
The whiche to me were hard now for to finde.
O goode God! how gentil and how kinde
Ye semed by youre speche and youre visage
The day that maked was oure mariage!

855 '*But sooth is seyd—algate I finde it trewe,*
For in effect it preeved is on me—
Love is noght oold as whan that it is newe.
But certes, lord, for noon adversitee,
To dyen in the cas, it shal nat bee

860 *That evere in word or werk I shal repente*
That I yow yaf myn herte in hool entente.

'My lord, ye woot that in my fadres place
Ye dide me streepe out of my povre weede,
And richely me cladden, *of youre grace.*

865 To yow broghte I noght elles, *out of drede,*
But feith, *and nakednesse, and maidenhede;*
And heere again your clothing I restoore,
And eek your wedding ring, *for everemore.*

Et voulentiers feray lieu a ta nouvelle femme, laquelle soit en ton boneur et aventure, comme de tout mon cuer le desire. Et de cy,[1] ou j'estoie et demouroie en grant plaisir, puis qu'il te plaist, voulentiers me partiray.

A quoy, toutesfoiz, me commande tu que je reporte avec moy mon douaire, quel il l'est je le voy, ne je n'ay pas oublié comment, quant pieça[2] tu me voulz prendre a femme,

je fus desvestue sur le seul[3] de mon pere des povres robes que j'avoye vestues, et fus vestue des tiennes grandes precieuses, ne en tout n'aportay avec toy autre douaire que foy et loyauté. Veez[4] cy, doncques, puis qu'il te plaist, je te desvests ceste tienne robe et rens l'aneau de quoy tu m'espousas.

---

[1] *cy* = ici.   [2] *pieça* = il y a longtemps.
[3] *seul* = seuil.   [4] *veez* = voyez.

'The remenant of youre jueles redy be
870 Inwith youre chambre, *dar I saufly sayn.*
Naked out of my fadres hous,' quod she,
'I cam, and naked moot I turne again.
Al youre plesance wol I folwen fain;
But yet I hope it be nat youre entente
875 *That I smoklees out of youre paleys wente.*

'Ye koude nat doon so dishonest a thing,
That thilke wombe in which your children leye
Sholde biforn the peple, in my walking,
Be seyn al bare; *wherfore I yow preye,*
880 *Lat me nat lyk a worm go by the weye.*
Remembre yow, myn owene lord so deere,
I was youre wyf, though I unworthy weere.

'Wherfore, in gerdon of my maidenhede,
Which that I broghte, and noght again I bere,
885 As voucheth sauf to yeve me, to my meede,
But swich a smok as I was wont to were,
That I therwith may wrye the wombe of here
That was youre wyf. *And heer take I my leeve*
Of yow, myn owene lord, lest I yow greve.'

890 'The smok,' quod he, 'that thou hast on thy bak,
Lat it be stille, and bere it forth with thee,'
But wel unnethes thilke word he spak,
But wente his wey, for routhe and for pitee.
Biforn the folk hirselven strepeth she,
895 And in hir smok, with heed and foot al bare,
Toward hir fadre hous forth is she fare.

Les autres aneaux, vestures, couronnes, et autres ornemens, que fortune m'avoit presté une espasse de temps
avec toy et, en faisant et paiant son deu, les me toust et
reprent, sont en tes escrins. Nue vins de chiez mon pere,
et nue la retourneray,

se tu ne repute et tien chose vil et malgracieuse, comme
je croy que tu feroyes, que ce ventre cy, qui a porté les
enffans que tu as engendrez, soit veu nus ne descouvert
au peuple.

Pour laquelle chose, s'il te plaist et non autrement, je te
supplie que, ou pris et pour la virginité que je apportay
avec toy, laquelle je n'en reporte mie, laisse moy une des
chemises que j'avoie quant j'estoie appellee ta femme.'

Lors ploura forment[1] de pitié le marquis si que a paine
contenir se povoit; et ainsi, en tournant son visaige, en
parler tout troublé, a paine peust dire, 'Doncques te
demeure celle que tu as vestue.' Et ainsi se party celle
sans plourer; et devant chascun se devesti, et seulement
retint la chemise que vestue avoit, et la teste toute des-
couverte et deschausse s'en va.

---

[1] *forment* = fortement.

97

The folk hire folwe, wepinge in hir weye,
And Fortune ay they cursen as they goon;
But she fro weping kepte hire eyen dreye,
Ne in this time word ne spak she noon.
Hir fader, that this tidinge herde anoon,
Curseth the day and time that Nature
Shoop him to been a lives creature.

For out of doute this olde poure man
Was evere in suspect of hir mariage;
For evere he demed, sith that it bigan,
That whan the lord fulfild hadde his corage,
Him wolde thinke it were a disparage
To his estaat so lowe for t'alighte,
And voiden hire as soone as ever he mighte.

Agains his doghter hastily goth he,
For he by noise of folk knew hire cominge,
And with hire olde coote, as it mighte be
He covered hire, *ful sorwefully wepinge.*
But on hire body mighte he it nat bringe,
For rude was the clooth, and moore of age
By dayes fele than at hire mariage.

Thus with hire fader, for a certeyn space,
Dwelleth this flour of wyfly pacience,
That neither by hire wordes ne hire face,
Biforn the folk, ne eek in hire absence,
Ne shewed she that hire was doon offence;
Ne of hire heighe estaat no remembraunce
Ne hadde she, as by hire contenaunce.

900 (line 900)
905 (line 905)
910 (line 910)
915 (line 915)
920 (line 920)

Et en cest estat la suivent plusieurs, plourans et maudi-
sans fortune, et elle seule ne plouroit mie[1] ne ne disoit mot.
Et ainsy s'en retourna en l'ostel de son pere.

Et le bon homs son pere, qui adés[2] avoit eu le mariage
suspet ne oncques n'en avoit esté seur, ains[3] doubtoit
tousjours que ainsy n'en avenist,

vint a l'encontre des gens a cheval sur son seul; et de
la povre robette, que tousjours lui avoit gardee, la couvry
a grant mesaise, car la femme estoit devenue grande et
embarnie[4] et la povre robe enrudiee et empiree.

Et demoura avec son pere par aucuns jours en merveil-
leusement grant humilité et pacience, si que nul signe
de tristesce, nulz remors de la prosperité qu'elle avoit eu
ne faisoit ne monstroit en aucune maniere.

---

[1] *mie* = à moitié. [2] *adés* = toujours.
[3] *ains* = mais. [4] *embarnie* = grosse.

GLOSSARY

abaised abashed, embarrassed
abaist disconcerted
abide (l. 119) wait for, stand still; (l. 1106) remain
abidinge enduring
abouten about
abreyde awoke, started
accepteth accept (imp.)
accident outward sign
acquite discharge, perform a part
adoun down
adversitee misfortune, calamity
after according to
again against
agains towards, to meet
agast frightened
ageyn again
agon dead, gone
agreved aggrieved, hurt
al entirely, although
alayes alloys
algate anyhow, none the less
alighte dismount
alliance marriage
also just as
alwey always, all the time
amende surpass
ameved moved, changed
angwissh anguish, distress
a-night at night
anon (l. 290) at once; (l. 435) for a while
aornementes adornments
apayed pleased
aperceive perceive, discern
aperceiveth observed, noticed

apertinent belonging to
apese pacify, settle
apparaille clothing, dress
arace tear away
archewives domineering wives or women
arn are
array (l. 262) order; (l. 273) state, condition
arrayed dressed, decked, made ready
arwes arrows, darts
as as if
aside to one side, apart
assay test, trial
assenten agreed
asseureth assure, give confidence (imp.)
astoned, -ied astonished, confounded
asure lapis lazuli
aswowne in a swoon, fainting
aton in agreement
atones at once, for all time
atte at the
atteyne attain, achieve
a-two in two
auctour author, writer
audience hearing
aventaille front of helmet
aventure (l. 15) adventure; (l. 812) chance, misfortune
avise deliberate, reflect
axe, axen ask
axeth requires, demands
ayeynes against
bachelrie young men, candidates for knighthood

bad commanded
badde bad, evil
bar (l. 85) bore, suffered; (l. 612) gave birth to
bareyne barren
barm bosom
bataille battle, fight
beede bid, offer
been are
beestes animals
benigne benign, gracious
benignely graciously
benignitee graciousness
berth bear
beste best, well-being
bete beaten
beth be (imp.)
bidaffed fooled
bifelle happened
bifoore before, previously
bigan began
bigile deceive
binde bind, put in bonds
biseke implore
bisekinge beseeching
biseye provided
bisinesse work, occupation
bisy anxious, worrying
bisynesse diligence, careful attention
bitake commit, entrust
bitide happen
bitwixe between
biwailled lamented
blisful happy
blisse bless
boghte bought, redeemed
boistously roughly
Boloigne Bologna
bord table
bore born
bounden tied

boundes limits, boundary
bountee goodness, virtue
boweth bend (imp.)
breste break
briddes birds
bringe bring, draw
broghten brought
bulles papal bulls
burieth bury (imp.)
but unless, except
buxomly submissively
caas case, affair
camaille camel
care be troubled
carie carry
cas event, occurrence
caughte (l. 619) was seized by; (l. 674) seized
certain for sure
certes assuredly
cesse cease, desist
chace pursue a narrative
chamberere (l. 819) mistress, concubine; (l. 977) chambermaid
chambre private room
charge (sb.) responsibility; (verb) command
charitee love, natural affection
chaunge alter
cheere (l. 7) appearance, behaviour; (l. 1112) good cheer, happiness
chese choose
cheste coffin
chiere appearance, face
chois choice
circumstance accompanying matter, accessory
clad dressed
cladden dressed

clappeth chatter (imp.)

clapping chatter, gossip

cleere bright, sparkling

clene chaste

clepe call, name

clerk, -es scholar, -s

cofre coffer, chest

collacioun conference, discussion

colours figures of speech

comaundeth gives order

commendinge praising, extolling

commune (adj.) common, general; (sb.) common people

compaignie company, presence

compleyned lamented

comth comes

comunly publicly

condicion nature, temperament

conforminge suiting, adapting

conjecture conclusion drawn from appearances

consaille advise

constance constancy

constreyned compelled, forced

contenaunce expression, composure

contree (l. 44) country, land; (l. 615) people of the country

conveyed accompanied, conducted

conveyen introduce

coote coat

corage (l. 220) mind, nature, disposition; (l. 628) courage, manly spirit; (ll. 692, 950) heart, mind; (l. 907) desire, will

corone, coroune wedding garland

costage cost, expense

cote humble cottage

couche cower, lie low

countrefete counterfeit, forge

countretaille point of retort, rejoinder

coy quiet, shy

crabbed bitter, ill-tempered

crepeth creeps

crien call upon, implore

crois cross

cures cares, employment, duties

curteisie courtesy

dar dare

day died

dede behaviour

deed dead

deeme, -n judge, suppose

deere dear, costly

deeth death

deface blot out, obliterate

defaute mistake, fault

degree social rank

delicaat (l. 682) delicate, dainty; (l. 927) pleasure-loving

delit pleasure

delitable delightful, attractive

desdeyne disdain, scorn

despitously cruelly

devise (l. 52) describe, relate; (l. 698) contrive

devisen imagine

devoir work, duty

deyde died

deye die

deyntee delightful, pleasurable

deyntevous choice, delicate

dide did

diffame disgrace, bad reputation

dighte prepare, make ready

digne worthy, honourable

diligence constant effort, endeavour

discreet wise, discerning

discriveth describes

dishonest dishonourable, shameful

disparage disgrace

dispence spending

dispende spend, pass time

dispensacion grant, licence

dispoillen strip, undress

disposed planned, decided

dissencion disagreement, discord

doghter daughter

doom judgement

doon, -e do, done

dooth does; do (imp.)

dore doorway

dorste dared

doun down

doutelees doubtless, of truth

dowaire dower, dowry

dowere dower, dowry

drad, -de feared, held in awe

drawe incline, move

dredde dread, fear

drede fear, anxiety

dreed fear

drery cruel, dire

dresse turn, address oneself to

dreye dry

dure last

dyen die

ech each, every, everyone

echoon each one, everyone

eek also, in addition

effect fact, result

egre fierce, sharp, bitter

eldres ancestors

elles else

emprenteth imprint, impress (imp.)

encresseth increases, widens

ende end, completion

endite write, compose

enditeth writes

endure bear, sustain

engendred created

enlumined shed lustre upon, rendered illustrious

enquere ask, enquire

entencion intention, design

entente meaning, purpose

entraille entrails, belly

equitee fairness, impartiality

er before

eres ears

ernestful serious

erst (l. 144) before; (l. 985) first

ese comfort, indulgence

esily happily, pleasantly

espie see

estaat condition, rank

evene tranquil

evere always, continually

everemo always, forever

everich every one

excercise spiritual trial, suffering

execucion carrying out of orders

experience proof by trial

eyen eyes

fader father

fadres (l. 61) ancestors; (l. 229) father's

fain gladly, willingly
fair good-looking, attractive
fairnesse beauty
falle (l. 259) belong, befit; (l. 938) happened
fame rumour, report
fane weather-cock, vane
fare gone
faste eagerly, industriously
fecchen fetch
feeste merriment
feet accomplishments
feithful constant, true
feithfully truly
felawes friends, companions
fele many
felicitee happiness
fer far
ferde behaved
ferme firmly
feste feast
fette fetched
fey faith
feyned pretended, feigned
feynting weakening, losing heart
fieble feeble, weak
figures figures of rhetoric
fil happened
fleeth flies away
flokmeele in a body
floure flourishes, blooms
folie lust, lasciviousness
folwen (l. 873) carry out, obey; (l. 1143) follow, imitate
folweth imitate (imp.)
fonde try, endeavour
foond found
forbede forbid
forgoon forgo, lose
fors matter, consequence

forth further
forther further, more advanced
fortunat prosperous
foryelde repay, reward
foryetful forgetful
foryeve forgive
fostre foster, bring up
fostred nurtured, brought up
foul ugly
fre generous, liberal
freendes friends
freletee frailty
freres friars
fresshe bright, vivacious
fro from
fulfild (l. 596) carried out; (l. 907) satisfied
fulliche fully
furlong short distance
game joke, pleasantry
gan did
geere belongings, clothing
gemmes precious stones
gentillesse good breeding, courtesy, nobility
gentilleste noblest, highest born
gentils gentlefolk
gerdon return
gesse suppose
gest guest
gete get, obtain
gide guide, conduct
glaade comfort, console
gladeth cheers, comforts
Goddes God's
gonne did
goost spirit
gooth go (imp.)
goth goes
governaille mastery, control

governance, governaunce rule, management, control

governeth decide, determine (imp.)

grace favour

gracious attractive, charming

graunten grant, allow

grauntmercy great thanks

grave bury

gree pleasure, good will

greet great

grene green, lively

grette greeted

gretter greater

greveth grieves

grucche grumble, complain against

gye guide, govern, direct

habundant fruitful

hadden had

halle public room

han have

hardily without hesitation, certainly

hardinesse courage, strength

hastif quickly arranged

hastily quickly

hauke hawk

heed head

heeld considered

heere hear

heeres head of hair

heeste command

heigh high

hem (l. 17) them; (l. 333) themselves; (l. 406) to them

hente seized

herbergage abode, home

herbes plants

herd, -e heard

herie praise, worship

heris hair

herkneth listen (imp.)

herte heart, courage

hertely heartfelt, sincere

hertes heart's

heste command

hevinesse sorrow

hewe complexion

highte (l. 32) was called; (l. 496) promised

hir their

hire her

holde (l. 273) directed; (l. 287) continues

holden considered

hond hand

honest decent, respectable

honestetee modesty, virtuousness

honurable worthy, distinguished

hool whole, entire

hoom home

hoomlinesse housekeeping

hooste host, innkeeper

houndes dogs

housbonde husband

humanitee compassion, benevolence

humblesse humility, meekness

hye high

idel idle, lazy

imagining pondering, considering

impertinent irrelevant

Inde India

inportable unbearable, insupportable

insight understanding

inwith within, in

Itaille Italy

ivel, -e evil, ill

jalousie jealousy

jane small Genoese coin
jueles jewels
juggement judgement
juggementz judgements
kan knows how to, can do, can
keep notice, heed
kembd combed
kesse kiss
kinde kindly, loving
knave boy, male child
knewe discovered, ascertained
konningly expertly, with experience
koude knew how to, was able to, could
kouth known
ladde led
lappe cloth wrapping
lasse less
last furthest point, remotest part
lat let
lauriat laureate, excellent, distinguished
leef leaf
leese lose
leeste least
leet let
leeveth believes, trusts
lenger longer
lest (sb.) wish, desire; (verb) pleases, wishes; wished, suited
lete abandon, forsake
lette delay
leve (sb.) permission; (verb) abandon, give up
levere rather
leye lay
leyser leisure

lief beloved
lige liege, subject
liken give pleasure
likerous lustful
liketh pleases
likinge wishes, inclination, pleasure
liklihede likelihood, probability
liklinesse appearance, semblance
limes limbs
linage descent, birth, family
linde lime-tree
list, -e pleased
lite little
litel little
lives living
livinge food, sustenance
lond country
longeth belongs
looking expression, appearance
loore learning, knowledge, experience
looth unwilling
lordinges gentlemen
lorn lost
lowely in lowly fashion
lulled soothed, sang to sleep
Lumbardie Lombardy
lust (sb.) (l. 80) liking, pleasure; (l. 214) sexual desire; (l. 531) will: (verb) like; pleases
lusty pleasant, vigorous
lyth lies
magnificence greatness, eminence, splendour
maide female child, girl
maidenhede virginity
maille mail-armour

maintene maintain, preserve

maistrie mastery, domination

make mate, partner

manaceth menaces, threatens

maner kind of

manere manner, conduct

mannes man's

maried married

markis marquis

markisesse marchioness

mateere (l. 55) subject-matter; (l. 90) affair, business

mazednesse stupefaction, dazedness

me myself

meede reward, return

meene mean

meeste highest, most distinguished

mekely meekly, humbly

melodie music

mente said, intended

merie joyful, pleased

merveille marvel, astonishing thing

merveillous astonishing, unaccountable

mesure (l. 256) measure, size; (l. 622) moderation

mete food

might utmost ability

mighte could

mirie pleasant, jolly

mo (l. 318) more; (l. 449) at other; (l. 1039) another

mooder mother

moot (l. 11) must; (l. 172) may

mordred murdered

moste might

mowe (l. 95) must; (l. 503) may

murie cheerful, pleasant

murmur complaint, discontent

murthe mirth, rejoicing

naille fasten down, restrain

namely especially

namoore no more, no further

nas was not

nat not

nathelees none the less, all the same

nay (l. 177) no; (l. 817) denial

ne nor, not

necligence carelessness, negligence

nede, -s needs, necessarily

nedelees unnecessarily, needlessly

nekke neck

nempned named, mentioned

nil (l. 119) will not; (l. 646) do not wish

nis is not

noblesse nobility, high rank

nobleye noble rank, splendour

noght (l. 78) not; (l. 84) nothing

nolde would not

noon (l. 123) no one; (l. 217) no; (l. 1071) neither

norice nurse

norissed brought up

norissinge upbringing

no thing, nothing not at all

noveltee unusual occurrence

nowches jewelled ornaments

ny near, nearly

o one

obeisance, obeisaunce obedience, submission

obeisant obedient

of off

ofte frequently, repeatedly

ofter more

oght anything
oghte (l. 132) ought;
    (l. 1120) befitted
on-lofte in being
oon one
ootherweys otherwise,
    differently
openly publicly
ordinaunce order, good
    arrangement
outrely absolutely, entirely
outreye fall into passion,
    become hysterical
outtreste furthest, extremest
outward material
overal in every respect
owene own
Oxenford Oxford
pace passes
Padowe Padua
paleys palace
paraventure by chance
parfitly perfectly
particuler particular, indi-
    vidual
passinge surpassing, excelling
pees peace
Pemond Piedmont
penible painstaking
perce pierce
persone body
peyne pain, penalty
peyned took pains, strove
pistel epistle
pitee pity, compassion
pitous (l. 97) sorrowful, sad;
    (l. 1080) tender, pitiful
place house
plentee abundance, plenty
plesance courtesy
plesaunce (sb.) pleasure;
    (verb) make happy

pley game
pleyn (l. 19) clearly, simply;
    (l. 926) simple
pleyne complain
plie bend
plowman ploughman, peasant
point condition
Poo Po
povre poor
povreliche in poverty
povrest poorest
precheth preach (imp.)
preeve (sb.) proof; (verb) test
preeved proved, exemplified
preeveth proves
preise -n praise, commend
prescience foreknowledge
presence company, gathering
preyde prayed, begged
preyere prayer, request
pridelees modest, without
    arrogance
prikke torment
pris value, excellence
privee attendant, confidential
    servant
prively secretly
privetee private place
profit good, well-being
profre offer
prohemie prologue
prudent judicious, discerning
publiced proclaimed, spread
    abroad
purveye provide
putten put
quaille quail
quakinge trembling
quod said
rancour ill-feeling, grudge
recchelees irresponsible,
    regardless of duty

rede (l. 811) advise; (l. 1154) read, study

redresse put right again

redy willing, prompt

reed (l. 317) red; (l. 653) advice, counsel

refuseden refused, ignored

rekke care

relesse release, remit

remenant remainder, rest

resoun reason, propriety

reste quiet of mind

restoore return, give back

retenue retinue, troop

rethorike rhetoric

retourneth return (imp.)

reule rule, conduct

reuthe pitiful sight

revel revelry, merry-making

reverence respect, veneration

rewen have pity

richesse lavish display

right (l. 243) veritable; (l. 1004) just

ripe mature

roghte cared

roially magnificently, splendidly

roialtee greatness, splendour

rome wander, travel

rood rode

roote foot

routhe compassion, pity

rude (l. 750) humble, poor; (l. 916) rough, coarse

rudely roughly

rudenesse humble conditions

rumbul rumour

sad serious, sober

sadly tenaciously, firmly

sadnesse steadiness, constancy

Saluces Saluzzo

saufly safely, with certainty

saugh saw

save except

say saw

scathe pity

sclaundre scandal, disgrace

secte sect

seelde seldom

seeth boiled

sely good, kind, hapless

semblant appearance

seme seem, appear

senden send, transmit

sentence opinion

servage servitude

serve, -de treat, -ed

servisable ready to do service

servise service, servitude

servitute servitude

sette adorned

seyde said

seyden said

seye say

seyn seen

shaltow you shall

shapen prepared, intended

shapinge making, directing

sharply spitefully, aggressively

shewe reveal, disclose

shewen make known

shilde forbid

shoon shone

shoop (l. 198) intended; (l. 903) disposed; (l. 946) contrived

shredde shredded, cut up

shul shall

siked sighed

sikerly assuredly, certainly

sikly with ill-will

sin since

sit suits, befits
site situation
sith since
sithe time
skile reason, cause
sklendre weak, without vigour
slake cease, die out
slaketh assuages
slawen slain
sleen kill
sleeth kills
sleighte cunning, dexterity
slide slip, pass away
smale slender
smerte (adv.) painfully;
  (verb) suffer, feel pain
smok smock, undergarment
smoklees without a smock,
  naked
smyt smites, strikes
sobrely gravely, seriously
sodeyn sudden, unexpected
softe softly
solempne ceremonious,
  splendid
somdeel somewhat
sondry various, varied
sonne sun
soore regretfully, sorrowfully
sooth true
soothfastnesse truth
soothly truly
sophime sophism, philo-
  sophical subtlety
souked sucked, been suckled
soun sound
sours source
soverainetee sovereignty,
  supremacy
sovereyn supreme, very great
space (l. 103) opportunity;
  (l. 918) space of time

spak spoke
special particular
specially in particular
speketh speak (imp.)
spille destroy, waste
spousaille wedding
spoused married
spradde spread
squieres squires
stalked walked slowly
stedefastnesse steadfastness,
  constancy
stente leave off, cease
sterres stars'
stert started
stidefast steadfast, constant
stierne stern
stille quiet
stinte stop, leave off
stondeth stand (imp.)
stoon stone
stoor store, reserve
stormy passionate, changeable
stounde moment
straunge unfamiliar, alien
streen stock, strain
streepe strip
strepeth strips
streyne press, force
strive resist
strook blow
studien study, deliberate
stuffed supplied, filled
sturdinesse cruelty, harshness
sturdy cruel
subgetz subject
subtil subtle, clever
subtiltee subtlety, cunning
suffisance contentment,
  happiness
suffisaunt capable, competent
suffise suffice, satisfy

Glossary

suffraunce patience, endurance
suffre allow, endure
suffreth allows
suppose think, believe
supposinge thinking, opinion
suspecious questionable
suspect (adj.) doubtful (sb.) suspicion
sustenance food, living
suster sister
swappe fall
swapte fell
swelwe swallow
swere swear, promise
swich such
swollen proud, haughty
swough swoon
swowninge swooning, fainting
taak take
t'affraye to frighten, alarm
t'alighte to demean, debase
t'amende to put right
t'assaille to attack
t'assaye to test, make trial of
teeres tears
telle describe, report
tempte make trial of, put to proof
tentifly attentively
termes technical expressions
thanke repay, reward
thanne then
that who
thenke intend
thenketh think, consider (imp.)
ther where
therbifoore previously, beforehand
therwith in addition

thewes morals, manners
thilke this, that
thing (l. 15) little story; (l. 52) matter
thinketh (it) seems
thise these
tho then
thogh although
thoght thinking, interest
thoghtful pensive, grave
thonken thanked
thoughte seemed
thresshfold threshold, doorway
throop thorp, hamlet
throwe short while
thurgh through
tidinge news
tigre tiger
to-morwe tomorrow
tonge tongue
tonne tun, barrel
torace tear to pieces
torent torn, tattered
tormentinge torture, cruelty
toun town
tour tower
translated transformed, changed
traunce trance, fainting-fit
travaille endeavour
tree wood
tretis contract
trewe true, sincere, constant
trewely truly
trouble disturbed, vexed
trouthe fidelity
trowe believe, suppose
trowed believed
trust expectation
tweye two
tweyne two

Glossary

equilibrium
disruption
recog. of disrupt.
attempt to repair
restoration
equilib.

ugly terrifying, repulsive
undertake warrant, dare say
undigne unworthy
undiscreet lacking discernment, ill-judging
undren noon, mid-afternoon (see note on l. 260)
unnethes hardly, with difficulty
unreste trouble
unsad unsettled, unstable
untressed unplaited, loose
untrewe inconstant
usage behaviour
vanitee folly, irresponsibility
variance difference, change
vermine beast of prey
verray true
vertu virtuousness
visage expression
vitaille food, provisions
voide quit, retire from
voiden send away, expel
vois voice
vouche sauf grant, permit
voucheth sauf permit (imp.)
waille lament, bewail
wantown wanton, lascivious
warne caution
wax became, grew
wedlok marriage
weede clothing, garment
weep wept
weere were
wel much
wele well-being, happiness
welkne heaven, sky
wend supposed
wende (l. 189) go, depart; (l. 544) thought, believed
went gone
wenten departed

werk actions, behaviour, achievement
werking actions, behaviour
wexe wax, increase
wey, *-e* path, road
whan when
whenne whence
whider whither
while time
whilom once, formerly
widwe widow
wight person
wikke wicked, evil
wil will, intent
wille (verb) desire, wish
willinge wishes, desire
winde fold about
wise fashion, manner
wisely heedfully, soberly
wiste knew
wit good judgement, wisdom, knowledge
withoute outside
witing knowledge
wive marry
wives wife's
wo grief, misery
wol *-e* will, wish to
wolde would
wolt wilt, will
wombe belly
wommanhede, *-heede* womanliness
wondre be astonished
woned accustomed
wont accustomed
woot knows
worm wretched creature
worshipe reverence, respect
worshipful respected
wortes edible plants, vegetables
wostow do you know

Glossary

woxen grown, become
wringe writhe
wroghte (l. 463) acted;
  (l. 1152) created, made
wrothe angry
wrye cover, clothe
wyfhood wifeliness
wyfly wifely, womanly
wys wise
wysly certainly, surely
yaf gave
yate gate
ybore born
yborn born
ydressed placed, set
ye eye
yee you
yelden yield, surrender
yerde rod, discipline

yeve give, grant
yeveth give (imp.)
yfeere together
yfeyned avoided by pretence,
  shirked
yfostred up brought up
yit yet, now
ylike alike
ynogh enough
yok yoke
yond yonder, out there
yoore (l. 68) for a long time;
  (l. 1140) long ago
youres yours
youreselven yourself
yow you
yprayed invited
yronne run, flowed
yset set, placed, appointed

Marie de France – two knights. Chaucer got story
from Petrarch & Petrarch got it from Boccaccio.

Divine seeds are sometimes rained down from
heaven into poor houses

- speculation over the nature of nobility
- Because Griselda is a peasant by birth & yet
behaves w such serene dignity we are in a
position to recognize that social rank is an
irrelevancy where true nobility of character
is concerned.

- Griselda has courage & adversity – feminine
constancy – submits themselves to God the same
way she did to her husband.

- innate nobility of Griselda compared w/ Christ
gathering water from well
- born in a peasants hovel grace of god 207
descended into a poor dwelling (ox's stall)
- Griselda's ready submission to suffering
- God "it is not fit for me into judge my supreme
wisdom – comparison w/ Walter

Griselda becomes humanised.

- Griselda represents perfect soul (Job) and Walter reflects God.

- The more realistic the story becomes the more we are outraged at the Tyrant. The tension between representational and literal is one the reader must work at for himself.

- It is complete within itself, but at the same time interconnected with the whole dialectic on marriage.

- Introduction of Grisel. intensifies religious symbolism

- she is pure, virgin, humble, obedient :: complying w/ rules of monastic life.

- she is symbolically washed (baptism) and led away while naked — she accepts Walter's challenge w/ christian fortitude + acceptance.

- when she returns home in a frock, this represents clear picture of solitary journey compared to Christ on the way to Calvary

- Griselda is spiritually superior, but socially inferior.

- " wifely submission is purely designed to flatter Walter's monstrous ego + does nothing for her saintliness.

- despite new exalted status she returns in her grey attire + gives unflinching obediance to her husband.